Engine
Management

Optimising carburettors, fuel injection and ignition systems

Haynes High-performance tuning series

Engine Management

Optimising carburettors, fuel injection and ignition systems

Theory

Planning

Installation

Calibration

Testing

Development

Maintenance

Troubleshooting

Engine mapping

Dave **Walker**

Technical Editor, *Cars & Car Conversions*

First published in August 2001
Reprinted three times in 2002
Reprinted in 2004 and 2005

A catalogue record for this book is available from the British Library

ISBN 1 85960 835 3

Library of Congress catalog card no 2001131348

Published by Haynes Publishing, Sparkford, Yeovil, Somerset BA22 7JJ, UK.
Tel: 01963 442030 Fax: 01963 440001
Int.tel: +44 1963 442030 Fax: +44 1963 440001
E-mail: sales@haynes.co.uk
Website: www.haynes.co.uk

Haynes North America Inc., 861 Lawrence Drive, Newbury Park, California 91320, USA.

Printed and bound in Britain by J. H. Haynes & Co. Ltd, Sparkford

All illustrations courtesy of the author except where credited.

WARNING
Whilst every attempt has been made throughout this book to emphasise the safety aspects of tuning engines, the publishers, the author and the distributors accept no liability whatsoever for any damage, injury or loss resulting from the use of this book. If you have any doubts about your ability to safely carry out any of the work described in this book then it is recommended that you seek advice from a professional engine tuner.

Jurisdictions which have strict emission control laws may consider any modification to a vehicle to be an infringement of those laws. You are advised to check with the appropriate body or authority whether your proposed modification complies fully with the law. The publishers accept no liability in this regard.

Contents

Foreword

It's about time Dave Walker wrote a book using his wealth of motoring knowledge and experience, and I was pleased to write a foreword for his first publishing foray. Dave has been Technical Editor of *CCC* for over a decade, and his technical/DIY features have helped many readers over the years to improve their road, race and rally cars. *CCC* is really the only monthly magazine in the UK that covers the technical aspects of performance motoring and motorsport in depth.

Engine management is an area of the motoring industry that has grown to the point where carburettors are almost, but not quite, obsolete. Dave is fortunate enough to have been around prior to the computer age – not to mention the Stone Age – and the section on carb selection and calibration was written from his own experience, not just cribbed from another book.

The engine management information came the same way – practical experience gained on Dave's famous rolling road and dyno. The software supplied with the book is a great help to those of us who don't have their own rollers. The simulated engine reacts just like an engine in the real world – if you ask it to do something that can't be achieved, it doesn't happen!

For tuning enthusiasts the software can be more fun and more rewarding than a Playstation, and if you haven't already moved with the times this book should help you into the new world of car tuning via the keyboard.

Steve Kirk
Editor *CCC*

Acknowledgements

I am indebted to a number of people, without whose help and encouragement I would not have been able to write this book.

Firstly, thanks to the late Leon Moss. Leon was a real no-nonsense Black Country engineer who had forgotten more about carburettors than I have ever learned. More than anything else, Leon taught me to *think*, not just accept.

Karl Paton, my engine-management electronics engineer, gets a big thank-you for patiently explaining complex electronics in terms that even I could understand. Without Karl I would never have got into engine mapping, and thus would have missed out on this fascinating subject area.

Thanks to John Robinson – Technical Editor of *Performance Bikes* magazine. John took me out of the workshop and into the world of editorials. I always tell people that from that day on I have never worked for a living – you can't call this work!

Lastly, I would like to thank all those of you who have read my editorial features over the years in *Motorcycle Mechanics*, *Car Mechanics*, *The Biker*, *Your Car*, *Fast Car* and finally, *Cars and Car Conversions* magazine. Without your readership I wouldn't have had a job that has allowed me to indulge in the tinkering which has led to this book. All I can say is that I hope that you find this book helpful, and that you are able to put the contents to good use.

Introduction

A close friend of mine once explained to me that the Motorsport Industry was not unlike the Computer Industry – they are both bullshit driven. It was the level of bullshit surrounding engine mapping and carburettor setting up that prompted me to write this book. There appears to be an almost endless supply of experts who can talk about the subject until the cows come home, but fewer people who can actually do a half-decent job.

The aim of this book is to provide the average motorsport enthusiast with enough theoretical knowledge to be able to make informed decisions, then to supply enough practical information so that those with access to the necessary equipment will be able to tackle the job themselves. Even if you can't tackle the whole job yourself, you should at least be in a position to tell if you are dealing with someone who can.

I have covered carburettor setting up in some detail because a lot of people think that this is something you can achieve in a couple of hours on a rolling road. Correct carburettor calibration takes longer than mapping, which is why so very few carburettor set-ups on amateur built engines are correctly calibrated. Another reason for the in-depth look at carburettors is that a lot of competition organisers still regard anything electronic as either black magic or 'expensive'. At the time of writing it has been something like ten years since a car equipped with a carburettor left any factory. Perhaps some people should move with the times?

PART 1
Before you start

Chapter 1

Engine checks

Introduction

Before you can attempt any kind of calibration, with either injection or carburettors, you have to know that the engine is basically healthy. Start with a visual inspection of the basics. Remember that rolling road or dynamometer time is expensive and you don't want to be spending money while you're adjusting tappets, dismantling cylinder heads or trying to stop your engine haemorrhaging oil.

Oil levels

Check the engine oil level; an engine that is over-filled can be just as much of a problem as one that is low on oil. If using a rolling road don't forget to check the gearbox and back axle oil levels too.

Coolant level

The coolant level should be correct, with no air locks in the system. Engines tend to run hotter

on a rolling road because the cooling fans do not produce the same air draught as you get at high speed on the road.

Oil leaks

Are there any oil leaks? If you can see oil where there shouldn't be any, don't just wipe it off!

Oil leakage can be a sign of crankcase compression forcing oil out through gasket joints or past oil seals. It may indicate loose

Fig. 1.1. Prior to setting-up, the engine needs to be run and checked for oil and water leaks.

components or simply poor attention to detail during assembly. Sort out any oil leaks before you go to the rolling road. If using an engine dynamometer, things are more difficult, but you can often use a make-shift stand to run the engine prior to bolting it to the dynamometer. You do not want to be paying a high hourly rate for someone to fix basic faults.

Compression check

Carry out a compression check to ensure that all the cylinders are basically sound. A cylinder leakage test should be made if you have any cause for concern. With a race engine, a variation in compression reading between cylinders of more than 5% needs investigation. The cylinder leakage test is more useful, in that you can listen for escaping air when a cylinder is down. This air may be coming back up the inlet tract, out of the exhaust, or via the breathers if compression is escaping past the piston rings. A new race engine will usually hold within 5% of

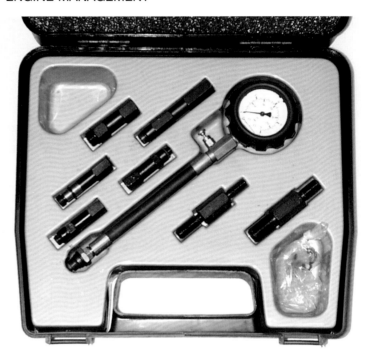

Fig. 1.2. A compression test before you start setting-up an engine will ensure that the engine is basically sound, and can save you a lot of setting-up time, and money, if there is a problem.

leakage at about 100psi. Anything much over 10% leakage needs to be investigated.

Fig. 1.3. A cylinder leakage test will pin-point the source of low compression, as well as giving a more realistic reading than a simple compression test.

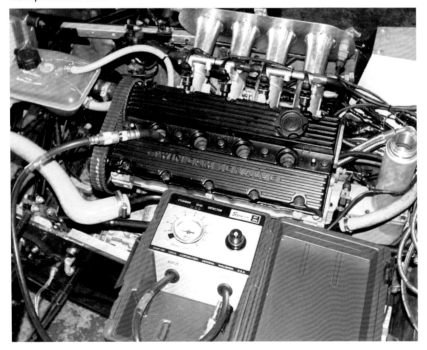

Air filters

The first bit of advice regarding air filters is simple enough – use them! You still see engines running with open intakes, often because the engine builder believes that an air filter restricts power. This is not the case. In fact, under certain circumstances you can gain power from fitting an air filter.

Actual filtration is also misunderstood. Many people think that competition air filters trap the dirt like a strainer or a sieve. They believe that air passes through the holes, which are too small for the dirt to pass through. This is not the case at all. Competition air filters, be they foam or cotton, work by being coated in a sticky oil. The air passing through the holes in the filter has the dirt removed from it because the dirt sticks to the oil trapped inside the filter. If the filter isn't oiled properly then its filtration ability is drastically reduced.

This is the main reason that competition filters need regular

Fig. 1.4. There's no excuse for not using an air filter. Power should not be affected – though it sometimes is!

Another consideration with air filters is the construction of the filter. Some filters allow air entry from all directions except the back-plate. Others have metal lids, which only allow air entry from the periphery of the filter. On initial inspection, the complete access filters look as if they would pass more air for a given size. But total airflow isn't the whole story. In Chapters 6 and 10, you can read about the pulse effect inside the induction system. Under some conditions that pulse can leave the intake bell-mouth and actually bounce off the air filter plate, changing the tuned length of the system. When you have a plate close enough to the intake for this to happen it is called a 'pulse plate'. For years, engine tuners have used pulse plates even when no air filter is fitted. The famous Ford GT40 Le Mans cars had such a device. As with tuning the bell-mouth length, pulse plates have to be experimented with. It's worth trying different width filters to see if they add power to your engine, rather than restrict it.

washing *and re-oiling*. The major filtration element is the oil, not the cotton or foam which holds the oil.

When most people shop for a filter, the first consideration is that it must fit the car. The bonnet, or hood, must close and not obstruct the free access of air. In an ideal world that air should be as cold as possible. Scoops, ducts and plain holes in the cover which allow cold air into the filter are all good news. Cold air is denser than warm air. Cold air therefore gives more power – *fact*.

Tyre pressures

Tyre pressures are very important on a rolling road. Use older tyres if

Fig. 1.5. Washing filters is supposed to be done with a special fluid, which does not attack the filtering medium.

Fig. 1.6. Air filters MUST be oiled if they are going to work. This applies to both cotton and foam types.

Fig. 1.7. A plate (known as a pulse plate) close to the intake trumpet can reflect the pressure wave and add to, or subtract from, the power.

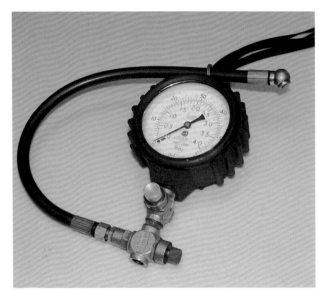

Fig. 1.8. Tyre pressures greatly influence the power-at-the-wheels reading. Make sure the pressures are correct before you start work.

you like, but make sure that they are up to transmitting the power from the engine. Damaged tyres should not be used for rolling-road work. A blow-out on the rollers is potentially very dangerous. If you are using a rolling road that only measures power at the wheels, keep the tyres for later repeat work, and note the tyre pressures. This is very important to maintain consistent results.

Chapter 2

Spark plugs

Theory and facts

Since the whole point of achieving the correct mixture is to burn it inside the combustion chamber to generate power, you are going to need a spark plug. In a high performance engine you must have the right plug, or all your tuning work will go to waste.

The spark plug has a fairly simple task. It offers a path to earth for the electricity produced by the coil. Within that earth path is an air gap, which the current must bridge in order to reach earth. When the current bridges the gap, a spark is produced, and this is the spark which starts the mixture burning. For such a simple device there has been endless nonsense published, claimed, and disputed, both about spark plugs themselves and about power outputs. First let's look at some facts.

Fact one: *You cannot get 'more' power from an engine by changing the spark plug. You can lose power by using the wrong plug, but recovering this lost power isn't a gain in the real sense.*

Fact two: *The make of plug has no bearing on power output. If the gap and the grade are exactly the same, the engine doesn't know which brand name is on the plug.*

Fact three: *Spark plugs with multiple earth electrodes offer a longer service life – nothing else. As one electrode wears down, the spark moves to the next nearest earth electrode.*

Fact four: *Precious metal plugs like platinum or iridium offer increased efficiency because the electrodes can be thinner and the*

gaps larger. This can reduce misfires and improve starting with cold/fouled spark plugs and rich mixtures. They do not produce more power.

Fact five: *You cannot 'improve' cylinder burning with a different plug design. Once the mixture is burning, the chamber shape and mixture movement determine how the mixture burns – the spark is long gone.*

Fact six: *The colour of the carbon on a spark plug tells you absolutely nothing about mixture condition. Only when you understand how a plug works can you use plug colour as a tuning aid.*

For a performance engine, the main criteria for plug selection is the heat range. Sitting inside the combustion chamber the plug naturally gets hot. The main

Fig. 2.1. Spark plug grade and type will influence the final result of tuning. Plugs do not make power!

Fig. 2.2. Multiple earth spark plug electrodes mean longer service life – nothing else.

Fig. 2.3. Rare-metal plug tips improve service life as well as spark generation.

G SERIES — 10mm .750" Reach 5/8" Hex

Heat	Regular	Retracted	Surface
HOT 69			
67			
65			
63			
61			
59	G59C		
57	G57C	G57R	
55	G55C	G55R	
			G54V
53	G53C	G53R	
			G52V
COLD 51			

J SERIES — 14mm .375" Reach 13/16" Hex

Heat	Projected	Proj Fine Wire	Regular	Fine Wire
69				
67			J8C	
65	RJ12YC		J6C	
63			J4C	
		J63Y	UJ81C	
61				J61
59				
57				
55				
53				
51				

A SERIES — 12mm .750" Reach 11/16" or 18mm Hex

Heat	Projected	Regular	Retracted	Surface
67	RA8HC			
65	RA6HC			
63	RA4HC			
61				
59		A59C		
57		A57C	A57R	
55		A55C	A55R	A55V
53		A53C	A53R	A53V
51			A51R	
			A50R	
49			A49R	

Fig. 2.4 Champion plug heat range chart.

cooling of the plug comes from heat being conducted through the plug's body and into the cylinder head. If the heat path is short the plug will run cooler, if the path is long it will run hotter.

Secondary cooling comes from the plug being in the path of the incoming fuel/air mixture. If the plug is well exposed to the incoming charge, this aids cooling. Plug position and electrode protrusion are the main elements which determine how much cooling effect the plug gets from the intake charge.

When the mixture burns it forms carbon deposits which cling to the cylinder head, and to the spark plug. If the carbon is not to bridge the air gap in the plug, it must be prevented from forming on the plug. You cannot stop carbon formation totally, but you can control it by allowing the plug to get hot. The heat will burn off the carbon and keep the plug clean. However, if the plug gets too hot it will cause a significant amount of damage to the engine.

If you are very lucky an overheated plug will simply melt the earth electrode, but in competition engines we cannot rely on luck. What happens in most cases is that the plug overheats and causes the mixture to ignite long before the spark arrives. This type of mixture ignition isn't a controlled burn, but more like an explosion inside the cylinder. We call this detonation, and it quickly destroys piston tops and piston rings, sometimes causing piston seizure in the bore. *An overheating plug is an engine killer.*

At the other extreme you can have a plug that never gets hot enough. A very cold running plug will quickly foul and stop working. It will make the engine difficult to start and you will get misfires. If a plug stops working and gets soaked in petrol it does not always respond to cleaning. Wet-fouled plugs can cause endless problems – throw them away!

With very highly tuned engines you may have need to start the engine on a hot-running plug and then fit the colder-running plugs once the engine has reached working temperature. Rich starting mixtures make life very hard for the cold-running spark plug.

Some companies produce race plugs. In many cases these plugs are of the 'surface discharge' type. This means that they do not have an earth electrode as such. The centre electrode is positioned relatively close to the outer body of the plug, and the spark jumps to the body to find its path to earth. There are many stories about race plugs and why they are designed this way. The principle reason for this design is that on very high-revving engines the vibration frequencies encountered can shake the earth electrode off a conventional plug design – this stops the engine firing on that cylinder. No earth electrode means no earth electrode to fall off. Life isn't always as complicated as some people would lead you to believe!

Reading spark plugs

Earlier I said that plug colour had nothing to do with mixture condition. What you are in fact looking at is the *temperature* of the plug, as indicated by the colour of the carbon formation. If you fit a hotter running plug the colour of the carbon will change to a lighter shade. This does not indicate a weak mixture, just a hotter running

Fig. 2.5 Tuning by plug colour. The colour indicates plug temperature, not mixture ratio

Normal – *Grey-brown deposits, lightly coated core nose. Plugs ideally suited to engine, and engine in good condition.*

Oil fouling – *Wet, oily deposits.*
Fault: *Worn bores/piston rings or valve guides; sometimes occurs (temporarily) during running-in period.*

Heavy deposits – *A build-up of crusty deposits, light-grey sandy colour in appearance.*
Fault: *Often caused by worn valve guides, excessive use of upper cylinder lubricant, or idling for long periods.*

Overheating – *Electrodes have glazed appearance, core nose very white – few deposits.*
Fault: *Plug overheating.*
Check: *Plug value, ignition timing, fuel octane rating (too low) and fuel mixture (too weak).*

Lead glazing – *Plug insulator firing tip appears yellow or green/yellow and shiny in appearance.*
Fault: *Often caused by incorrect carburation, excessive idling followed by sharp acceleration. Also check ignition timing.*

Electrode damage – *Electrodes burned away; core nose has burned glazed appearance.*
Fault: *Pre-ignition.*
Check: *For correct heat range and as for 'overheating'.*

Carbon fouling – *Dry, black, sooty deposits.*
Fault: *Over-rich fuel mixture.*
Check: *Mixture settings, cold-start fuelling, air filter.*

Split core nose – *May appear initially as a crack.*
Fault: *Detonation or wrong gap-setting technique.*
Check: *Ignition timing, cooling system, fuel mixture (too weak).*

plug. If you fit a colder running plug the carbon will be darker, even sooty in appearance. The mixture is not richer, it's just the plug running colder.

However, a richer mixture *will* cause the plug to run colder, while a weaker mixture will make it run hotter. If, and only if, the plug grade is known to be correct can you use the colour of the plug as a mixture indicator. Trying to tune on plug colour can be very misleading if the plug grade isn't correct for the engine. Some people work it the other way around. They optimise the mixture on the dyno and then change spark plug grades until they get the right colour – indicating the right heat range.

Plug terminology

There can be some confusion about plug terminology – hotter/colder and harder/softer grades. Manufacturers tend to use the terms hotter/colder to describe how their plug grades work. A colder plug is one that runs colder in the combustion chamber. For competition use we tend to look towards colder running plugs to cope with our highly tuned engines. The plug must run hotter if we rev the engine higher. With an engine running at 8000rpm we have twice as many burn cycles, within the same time frame, as we do at 4000rpm – the plug will run hotter if we don't select a colder-running grade. Some engine tuners talk about harder/softer plugs. In this case harder means colder running and softer means hotter running. If we all stop using this harder/softer plug terminology life will get less complicated for all of us!

Chapter 3

Cam timing

Theory

Mapping is just part of setting up an engine. Cam timing is critical to getting the best from any set-up, be it carburettors or injection.

The traditional method of cam timing with a dial gauge on the valve and a degree disc on the crankshaft is complete and utter madness. Only a fool would go to all this trouble when there is a far simpler, *and more accurate* method of setting up the camshaft. Also with the engine fitted into the car it is often impossible to fit a degree wheel to the crankshaft. If you can fit the wheel, in most cases you won't be in a position to read it.

First of all let's consider what you are trying to achieve with camshaft timing. Obviously you want the best from the cam in terms of engine performance, but what does the engine 'see' with different cam timings? The answer in the main is that the engine reacts to the lift on overlap of the inlet and exhaust valves. When the cam grinder fits the blank into the machine to grind the lobes, he will dial in a lobe centre angle. This is the angle between the two sets of lobes, inlet and exhaust. A common angle is 110°. If the grinder uses this angle he will specify full lift at 110° of crankshaft rotation, putting the camshaft dead centre at 55° (half the crankshaft number allows for the 2-to-1 gearing of the cam drive). This sets the cam to exactly equal lift on both inlet and exhaust at TDC. If the lobe centre angle is closed up, perhaps to 108° to increase lift on overlap, the grinder will specify 108 crankshaft degrees for full lift at the valve.

Basically what you are trying to achieve is equal lift on overlap at TDC. So why not simply measure it and adjust the cam accordingly? With asymmetric cams it is

Fig. 3.1. The Lobe Centre Angle (LCA) determines the valve lift on overlap, which is the critical setting when timing the camshaft.

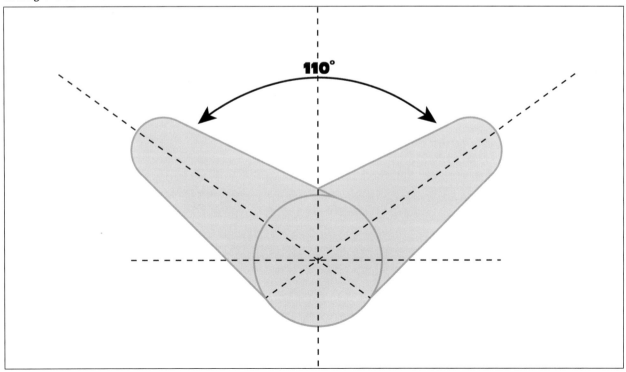

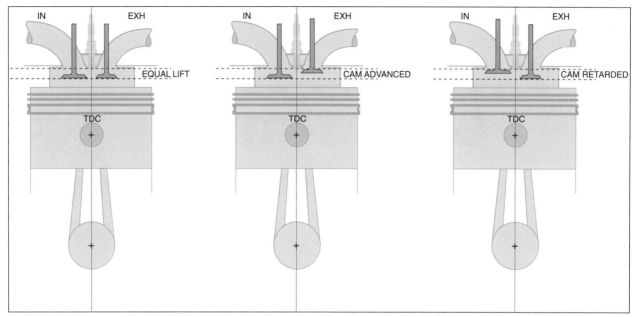

Fig. 3.2. Using valve lift on overlap, you can set cams up accurately without the need for a timing disc on the crankshaft.

possible that timing the cam to the lobe centre angle will not give equal lift on overlap, but that's just another reason for not timing the cam in at full lift. What the engine is seeing is the valve open positions relative to the piston position around TDC, so this is the only accurate way to time in the cam. It takes into account non-symmetrical cams, odd rocker ratios and slightly inaccurate cam grinding or tappet setting.

If you are trying to set up an unknown engine, it is much easier to measure valve lift on overlap than to try fitting a degree wheel to the engine. In most cases you can put a magnetic clamp on the engine, first bolting on a steel plate if the head is aluminium. A dial gauge can usually be positioned accurately enough if you use some welding rod, bent into a convenient extension. In an ideal world you would use two gauges, one on the inlet, one on the exhaust. Most of us only possess one gauge and stand so this has to be transferred from inlet to exhaust. Fortunately this isn't a major operation.

What you will have to do is check the TDC marks on the crankshaft. Manufacturers give you

a TDC pointer system on most engines, but sometimes people put their own marks on the pulley, or change the pulley for one that has no TDC mark on it (when using a toothed-belt drive pulley for example). If at all possible, remove a spark plug, put a rod down the plug hole and feel for TDC as the engine is slowly turned over. Ideally, you should use a dial

gauge with an adapter screwed into the pug hole, but many eight-valve engines have angled plugs and this isn't practical. If you can't get an exact mark, don't worry. You can optimise the cam timing by taking power curves. Get the TDC mark as close as you can and then you at least have a reference.

To measure the valve lift on overlap of a built engine, simply

Fig. 3.3. You will need an accurate TDC mark on the crankshaft pulley.

Fig. 3.4. A dial gauge on the valve measures the amount that the valve is lifted off the seat.

position the engine at TDC and place your dial gauge on the inlet valve on the cylinder that is on overlap. Zero the gauge and turn the engine backwards until the inlet valve closes. Note what the lift had been at TDC. Reset the engine to TDC and put the dial gauge on the exhaust valve. Zero the gauge and rotate the engine forwards until the exhaust valve is fully closed. Note the lift and then compare the two figures.

To time the cam to the 'as ground' figure you need to adjust the timing until both valves have equal lift at TDC. On a single-cam engine this means rotating the cam either way as necessary until you get the valve lifts equal.

On a twin-cam engine it's more complicated, because you can adjust either cam individually. The big advantage is that you can alter the angle between the cams to increase lift on overlap, or decrease it. If your engine has already been running, and you are simply setting up on the rolling road/dyno, then I would suggest splitting any difference in lift as a starting point. Work as though the engine had a

single cam. For example, if the inlet is reading 0.120in lift and the exhaust is 0.030in, you have two choices. You can reduce the inlet or increase the exhaust to get equal lift. I would suggest taking the average and setting both valves to 0.075in of lift at TDC.

Once you start taking power curves on a twin-cam engine, you can increase lift on overlap, reduce it, or move both cams, to find the optimum position. If you advance or retard both cams, rather than moving the cams individually, the effect is an overall advance or retard.

Vernier pulleys

Some people install cams without adjustable pulleys. On belt-driven engines this isn't a big problem. The cam pulleys will almost certainly be located with a Woodruff key. Leave the key out. Simply set the cam(s) to the required position and then fit the pulley(s), adjust the timing belt tension and bolt up the pulley(s). The Woodruff key does not provide the drive for the cam, it is the clamp on the shaft which takes the drive.

Many engines, like the Ford Zetec, do not have any locating key-ways as standard. You use a setting tool to position the cams and then tighten the pulley retaining bolts. As long as the bolts don't come loose, the timing will not creep. I use Loctite on the bolt threads, having thoroughly cleaned them beforehand. If you make a hash of it and the bolt comes loose, you will bend all the valves and damage the pistons – you have been warned! Everyone must take responsibility for their own actions.

The biggest advantage of an adjustable pulley is that it allows you to move the cam, and then recover the original position if you don't like the results. In an ideal world you will already know the limits of cam adjustment before you bring the valves too close to the pistons. If assembling the engine prior to testing, you have the opportunity to find the limits during the build stage, as follows.

I assemble the valves in one cylinder-head chamber, fitting them with very light springs. Install the cam and valve operating gear and set the tappet adjustment, then fit the head. Bring the checking cylinder to top dead centre (TDC) and set the cam to the lift-on-overlap position. Move the cam until both inlet and exhaust valves are partially

Fig. 3.5. A simple way to experiment with cam timing is to remove the locating Woodruff key. See text for details.

Fig. 3.6. Light springs allow you to check the amount of piston-to-valve clearance you have at different cam timing settings.

Fig. 3.7. The dial gauge tells you the distance between the valve, the piston, and disaster!

open by the same amount, with the piston below at TDC. Connect the drive belt/timing chain and tension it, locking the vernier pulley or tightening the pulley nut, as applicable. Now put a dial gauge on the valve cap and press down the valve by hand. Watch the dial gauge to see how much valve travel you have before the valve makes contact with the piston. Transfer the dial gauge to the other valve and make the same check. The valve-to-piston clearance may not necessarily be the same for both inlet and exhaust valves at this stage.

Now you need to rotate the engine a few degrees and re-check the clearance. Depending on the stroke of the engine, the connecting-rod length and the cam-lifting ramp design, you may well find that the valve-to-piston clearance reduces slightly as the piston swings across TDC. What is happening is that the valve is opening faster than the piston is moving away from TDC. There are no set rules, you simply move the engine backwards and forwards until you find the spot where the clearance is tightest. Make a note of the clearance and then check the other valve/valves for the cylinder in question.

In a perfect world you only need to check that nothing actually

touches. In reality you have to have sufficient clearance to allow for some valve float in the event of an over-rev. How much clearance will depend on the valve-spring rate and how the installed spring pressure is set up. If the valve spring goes coil bound at 50thou (0.050in) more lift than the cam gives it, then theoretically you only need 51thou (0.051in). But then you have to allow for rod stretch at high rpm, metal expansion, and tappets closing up in service. A sensible minimum clearance to aim for is 120thou (0.120in) or 3mm, but this

figure is for guidance only, at the end of the day *you* are building the engine, not me. I often run my engines down to a clearance of 50thou (0.050in). Sometimes I clip a valve on over-rev!

Now you can move the cam timing a few degrees and repeat the check all over again. What you have to discover is how far advanced, or retarded, you can move the cam before you get too close to the piston-to-valve contact point. If this work is done now, you can swing the cam timing on the rolling road or dyno later without

Fig. 3.8. Incorrect cam timing caused this disaster! Measure and note piston-to-valve clearances during the engine build.

Fig. 3.9. The CVH engine needs relatively little increase in valve lift-on-overlap to get impressive power gains.

Fig. 3.10. This Pinto combustion chamber likes a lot of lift-on-overlap to produce 100bhp/litre.

having to worry about going too far either way and damaging the engine. It also helps to know if you can move the cam in an area where you are likely to make gains.

Cam timing advance/retard works like this. When both valves are open by the same amount at TDC you have zero cam timing, neither advanced nor retarded. When you have more inlet valve lift than exhaust valve lift, the cam is advanced. When you have more exhaust valve lift than inlet valve lift, the cam is retarded. Quite often people install a cam by the full lift/crankshaft degree method and get it wrong, leaving the cam advanced. When they dyno test and discover that moving the cam back towards retard picks up power, they state that the cam works better retarded. I have never found a cam which works better when truly retarded, with more exhaust lift than inlet at TDC, but there's always a first time – I wait to be surprised.

Let's look at some numbers. Measure the lift-on-overlap of a standard camshaft, and you could well find that there is almost no lift-on-overlap at all. Modern emissions-conscious engines run very little overlap, but still make good power. Overlap only really works with a tuned-length exhaust system. Taking the 1600cc Ford CVH engine as an example of a two-valve

design, the standard engine runs something like 10thou (0.010in) of lift on overlap at TDC. With an otherwise standard engine you can increase duration, lift-on-overlap and maximum lift and you gain absolutely nothing at all, other than extending the rev range slightly. With engines running the standard K-Jetronic Bosch injection (mechanical, not electronic) you will have severe running problems if you fit larger-overlap camshafts. The air-metering flap gets very confused by reverse pulses in the inlet – which is why the injected CVH has so little lift-on-overlap as standard. However, if you fit a carburettor, or electronic injection, then port the cylinder head and remove the inlet restriction, you get impressive gains with lift-on-overlap of up to 60thou (0.060in) on both valves at TDC. Going over this point with the 'hemi' combustion chamber design only results in a loss of tractability, giving less low-speed torque with no gains at the top end.

Now look at the Ford Pinto 2.0 litre engine. This has massive ports as it leaves the factory. On a race-built engine you can run up to 200thou (0.200in) of lift-on-overlap on both valves and get just over 100bhp/litre from the engine. It all depends on the engine design and the modifications that you need to make in order to get the best from

the cam. Remember, the camshaft is only part of the equation, everything must work together.

Power curves

Fine tuning of the cam timing takes place after you have set up the fuelling and the ignition timing. Take a power curve with a known cam timing setting and then retard the cam slightly. Theory says that this will give you an increase in top-end power at the expense of the mid-range. This seldom, if ever, happens in the real world. Often there is just one sweet spot that the engine likes, and moving the cam either way just reduces power everywhere.

Take a second power run with the cam in the new position and then compare the two curves. It's often more informative to look at the torque curves than the bhp curves. You have to swing the cam and compare curves, looking for the shape of torque curve that best suits your needs. Sometimes gaining a couple of bhp at peak revs just isn't worth the trade-off in terms of lost mid-range torque.

Once you have the torque curve optimised from moving the cam timing, you may have to look at the ignition timing again or the fuelling, on a mapped system using throttle position as the main load reading parameter.

Chapter 4

The knock

Knock, knock – who's there?

In order to gain a more complete understanding of engine calibration, we need to look in some depth at the type of fuel we are using and how it affects the way we set up the engine.

The main criteria for mapping, or carburettor jetting, is that the engine delivers the best possible power without destroying itself! The ability of the engine to live a useful life will depend to a large extent on the fuel that we use. It isn't uncommon for people to turn up at the rolling road with a tank full of low-octane unleaded. You can set up the engine on this fuel, but it isn't going to give anything like the power you'll get from a higher-octane petrol. Let's first look at how the octane rating of the fuel affects the engine.

As we have already stated, the fuel and air mixture burns in a *controlled manner* inside the combustion chamber, starting at the spark plug and radiating from there. If that combustion isn't controlled, we get 'knocking' noises coming from the engine. There is a lot of confusion about engine knocking noises, so let's look at the three most common sources of unwanted noise.

Pinking

This is the most common noise of all, and it produces a light metallic clinking sound. Pinking is actually caused by the ignition being too far advanced. What happens is that the pressure rise in the cylinder occurs too early, and the piston rattles against the bore as it goes over TDC. This is a mechanical rattle and it has nothing to do with combustion. Pinking at light load and low speed isn't an engine breaker, in fact it is quite harmless as long as it is not allowed to continue for too long. Since you will gain both power and peace-of-mind by retarding the ignition at this point, there's no excuse for living with it.

Knock

Inside the combustion chamber, as the flame front spreads out from the spark plug, a series of reactions take place in the gases ahead of the flame front. We call the gases that are furthest from the plug 'end gases', and under certain conditions these end gases can auto-ignite. In place of the smooth burn, we now have two flame fronts, which collide and produce a knocking sound. This noise is much heavier than the light pinking previously described.

Exactly when this knock can take place will depend on many conditions within the engine; mixture ratio, ignition timing, compression ratio, spark plug position and combustion chamber shape being just a few. The main factor though is the fuel's ability to resist knock. Different fuel additives can reduce the tendency for the end gasses to auto-ignite, and so the controlled combustion reaches the end gasses before they auto-ignite.

In the early days of the internal combustion engine engineers

Fig. 4.1. The octane rating of the fuel is determined by this monster – the single-cylinder research engine.

wanted to find a way of rating a fuel's ability to resist knock, and they came up with the octane rating system. What they actually came up with was a single-cylinder research engine with a variable compression ratio. They had two base fuels – one which was very knock resistant, and one which wasn't. The poor fuel was heptane, and the good stuff was iso-octane.

Using the research engine, you run your test fuel until knock sets in. The engine is equipped with a meter to measure the degree of knock present. You adjust the engine so that you get an average knock value, and then you run the engine again on a blend of heptane and iso-octane, and compare the results. When you get a blended fuel that matches the test fuel, you give the test fuel an octane number corresponding to the proportion of iso-octane in your blended fuel. For example, a test fuel that matched a blended fuel with 95% iso-octane would get a 95 octane rating.

Since knock occurs more readily at low speed, the engine was first run at 600rpm for the test. The octane rating measured was known as the 'research octane number' or RON. But it was soon found that this didn't have much bearing in the real world under heavy load conditions, so another test was done under similar conditions but at 900rpm. The result from this later test was known as the 'motor octane number' or MON. To arrive at the octane rating which we find on a forecourt fuel pump, we take both RON and MON numbers and then average them.

In general, the RON number tends to be higher than the MON number, and it is the MON number that is of more interest to the performance minded, since we tend to run at high speed under heavy load conditions more often than under light cruise conditions. As you can see, there is more to this octane rating business than first meets the eye.

Additives can be put into the fuel to increase the octane rating. Lead was an excellent additive, and it is amusing to note that when lead first appeared, the oil companies charge a little more for it. Years later, when they removed it again, they charged a little more for taking it out!

Pre-ignition

Sometimes referred to as 'detonation', this isn't a noise you have to put up with for very long. Very soon after it appears, pre-ignition will kill the engine stone dead.

Pre-ignition means that the fuel and air mixture starts to burn before the spark arrives. This is caused by something in the combustion chamber getting hot enough to ignite the fuel mixture. You hear a lot of talk about carbon deposits, but for a race engine it's almost always the spark plug overheating that causes pre-ignition to take place.

Spark plug overheating may be caused by having the wrong plug grade (see 'Spark plugs'), but it is more commonly caused by ignition timing which is too far advanced, and/or a weak mixture. The increased combustion temperature caused by advanced ignition or a weak mixture causes the plug to overheat, and pre-ignition/detonation takes place. The plug is almost always the source, even if it isn't the cause.

An engine that is detonating for even a short time period will destroy pistons, rings, valves and spark plugs. It often appears as if someone has taken a welding torch to the piston, with enough aluminium burnt way to enable you to see all the piston rings through the hole in the piston! It's difficult to describe the difference in noise between pinking, knock and pre-ignition, but if you have any degree of mechanical sympathy, it can best be summed up as: pinking will make you concerned, knock will make you wince and detonation will make you cringe!

Chapter 5

What is power?

The theory

You hear a lot of bar-room talk about bhp, but how many of those involved in such deep discussions actually understand the numbers that they are quoting? One bar-room expert will brag about his maximum bhp number, while another (claiming to be wiser) will tell you that what really matters is torque. They are talking about two different things. If you think of torque as the *effort* that your engine is making, then bhp is the actual *work* that gets done. If you struggle to lift a heavy weight, but fail in the attempt, you have expended a lot of effort. But by not moving the weight you have singularly failed to do any work!

When the mixture inside an internal combustion engine burns, the pressure rise in the cylinder forces the piston down the bore. That pressure is transmitted through the connecting rod, which in turn rotates the crankshaft. The crank spins the flywheel, and we have a running engine. If you could take hold of the flywheel and hold it still, the force trying to make it rotate is the torque which the engine produces. While we can't hold the engine still to measure the torque, we can measure the resistance needed to hold the engine at any given rpm. The machine used to hold the engine at the required rpm is called a dynamometer (dyno), or engine brake.

Using this method, we are then measuring the *average* torque that the engine is producing. Since work is force multiplied by distance, we need to multiply that force, or torque reading, by the distance (engine rpm). From this we can see that a given torque figure will translate to a higher bhp number if the torque is produced at higher rpm. So what exactly is bhp?

Let's go back a few hundred years. Before the invention of the infernal combustion engine everyone used animals to provide motive power. The most popular working animal was the horse. When engines first appeared, people wanted to relate their power to a known value, ie the horse. One engineer figured that a horse could move a 33,000lb load over a distance of one foot in one minute. Or, this mythical horse could move 1650lb a distance of 20ft. In each case, the work done is exactly the same; force multiplied by distance moved in one minute. This is our standard 1 bhp today. Since the engine's torque was measured on a braking device, the power was called Brake Horse Power (bhp). The only engine value that we can measure on a dyno or rolling road is torque. The bhp is calculated from the torque reading and the engine rpm. The equation looks like this:

$$bhp = \frac{2 \times Pi \times torque \text{ (ft lbs)} \times rpm}{33,000}$$

Since 2 x Pi is a constant this can be reduced to:

$$bhp = \frac{Torque \times rpm}{5252}$$

Therefore:

$$Torque = \frac{bhp \times 5252}{rpm}$$

If you have one value, you can then calculate the other, and both bhp and torque will be the same at 5252 rpm. Now that we understand what we are measuring, we can look at how we measure it. Let's start with the machines most commonly used, the dynamometer (dyno) and the rolling road.

Dynomometer and rolling road – how they work

The chances that you will own a rolling road or an engine dyno are pretty remote, but that doesn't mean that you've no need to know how they work. A good basic understanding will help you to select your rolling road or dyno cell operator from a position of strength, not ignorance.

The first engine brakes, either rolling road or dyno cell, used water as the drive medium. To use one of these early machines, you connect the engine to one paddle wheel and the load measuring scales to another. As the engine rotates, the first paddle wheel churns the water, which presses on the second paddle wheel. You adjust the flow between the two paddles until you have the desired engine rpm, and then measure the torque – in the early days with a spring scale. We call this set-up a Water Brake.

Then came the eddy current brake. This is really just an electric motor that is driven by the engine. An electric current is then fed into the motor, to try to make it rotate in the opposite direction. When the right amount of current is fed in, the two forces are balanced and the engine rpm holds steady. This is an Eddy Current Brake.

The next major improvement in engine brake technology was the invention of the electronic load cell. Rather than using a spring scale, you have a load cell which measures the torque passed from the engine brake into an arm. The cell reacts instantly and gives an electronic reading which can be displayed on a read-out, or fed directly to a computer. Computers can capture data much faster than the human eye, and this means that you can record complete power curves with relative ease.

To alter the rpm of a water brake you need to adjust the paddle system. This involves moving gates to control the water flow, which can be done with a large wheel, a lever, or with a geared electric motor. Either way it's a fairly slow process with most water brakes, and it involves some effort. With an eddy current brake you can alter the current flow in the blink of an eye and with very little effort. Because eddy current brakes are so fast to respond, they have some big advantages over a water brake. For example, you can set the engine rpm with the engine at half throttle, then open the throttle, and the electronics will hold the engine rpm at the same point. With a water brake, opening the throttle will increase the engine rpm until you adjust the gates to bring the rpm back to the starting point. This doesn't sound like much of a hardship for the water brake operator, but it's a massive disadvantage if you are mapping an engine. With the speed and load fixed, you can alter the ignition and mixture settings to optimise them. Every time you get a gain in torque, the engine rpm tries to move and you then move off that speed and load site to a different setting. You then have to bring the rpm back to the mapping point and make another adjustment. You can chase round in circles like this for some time before you can be satisfied that you have achieved optimum

mapping for that one site.

With an electronic eddy current brake the engine rpm stays the same whatever the torque output, so you can adjust the fuel and ignition settings very quickly by watching the torque reading. The engine will not move off site as you make improvements. This is the *single biggest advantage* of the electronic eddy current brake.

The second advantage of the electronic eddy current brake is that you can measure the engine torque as the engine accelerates. A computer program can control the load on the dyno to allow the engine to accelerate at a given rate. The load cell captures the torque and you can get a complete power curve just by accelerating the engine from low rpm to high rpm in one go. This is a very useful facility for checking the whole power curve and, if the computer software allows you to lay one curve over the other, comparisons can be made very quickly in order to evaluate small changes in engine tune.

With the advent of computers we now have a third type of dyno – the inertia dyno. This is a rolling road with a single roller of a known mass. This machine is pretty accurate since it's just a lump of mass, and a computer calculates the work done in accelerating, and decelerating, it. The computer doesn't know where the power is coming from, it just reads the power as work done – or undone. You strap the car down and accelerate on full throttle, or fixed part throttle if you like. The computer produces a power curve, which is calculated by timing how long it takes for the roller to accelerate, and then decelerate again.

With an inertia dyno you cannot hold any given rpm value or alter the throttle load during a run. All you can do is measure a power curve under acceleration conditions, and the acceleration rate is fixed. The system is accurate and there isn't much to go wrong with it, but it has very limited use in

terms of setting up an engine, and for accurate mapping it is a waste of time.

Dyno or rolling road?

The biggest advantage of the dyno cell is that you are measuring torque directly from the crankshaft. You can also control air temperature inside the cell, coolant temperature inside the engine, and even air pressure in come cells, which keeps you completely in the picture as to how the engine is performing under carefully controlled conditions.

The biggest disadvantage of the dyno cell is that the engine is not operating under the same conditions as it will in the car. Quite often the engine is fitted with a different exhaust, seldom silenced. With a rolling road the engine is running in exactly the conditions under which it will operate in the car. You have the car's induction system, bonnet, bulkhead and cooling system in place. This is the real world as far as the engine is concerned.

The main disadvantage of the rolling road is that you are

Fig. 5.1. An engine set up ready to run on a dynamometer.

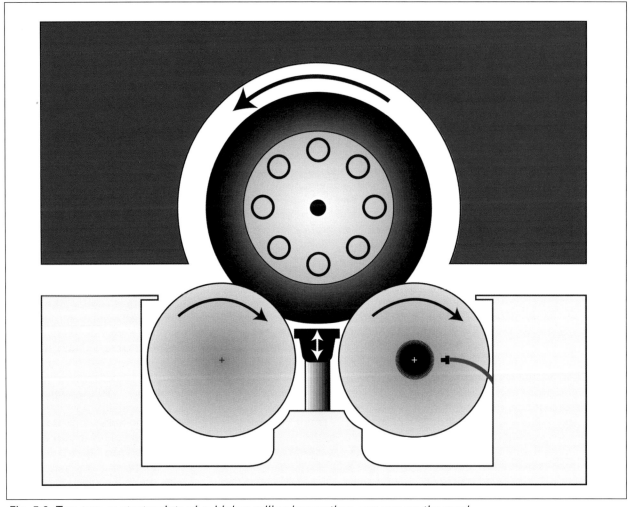

Fig. 5.2. Two tyre contact points give higher rolling losses than you see on the road.

measuring the torque at the road wheels, not straight off the engine. This means that the final power at the road wheels will be affected by the transmission system operating conditions, such as any clutch slip, or oil drag in the box or axle, and by the rolling resistance of the tyres. This does not give a direct picture of what is happening at the engine, neither is it a direct picture of what happens on the road.

On the road you have one compression 'flat spot' where the tyres meet the road. On a rolling road you have two compression flat spots. Having a pair of rollers pressing against the road wheels really does introduce some unrealistic losses into the picture, in that you have an unnatural degree of compression of the tyre wall brought about by a relatively small diameter roller. What's more, you have two contact patches of a concave nature clouding the issue further. If the rolling-road operator is very keen and puts a strap on the back of the car to pull it down onto the rollers, it gets really interesting! If a car needs that level of grip, it generally has a very powerful engine, which in turn means big (wide) tyres. The bigger/wider the tyre, then generally the more energy it takes to compress the side-wall. You don't have to be a genius to work out that the faster you go, the more effort it takes to keep deforming the side-wall (same deflection but in an increasingly smaller time-frame), hence 'total rolling losses' increase with road speed.

The only way to accurately map/set up an engine is with it installed in the car in which it is to be used, and so a rolling road will give the best results, provided the operator is skilled and able to interpret the results.

Fig. 5.3. The wider the tyre the higher the rolling losses.

Using a rolling road

Of course, there are different types of rolling road, and they can be set up in different ways. My own Sun RAM12 has the facility for holding a given road speed – regardless of engine applied load. To use this facility, you dial in the road speed, and when the car gets to, for example, 60mph, it won't go any faster. You can increase throttle until the tyres spin and smoke, but the brake holds the rollers at 60mph, regardless of what gear you are in. This is very useful for mapping, as already mentioned, where you need to hold a steady load and speed in order to play with the fuel and ignition settings. On my rollers I have a digital read-out, which reads to within 0.1 of a bhp. When you tweak the ignition timing on the lap-top, you can see small changes which, while not deadly accurate, do give you an indication of what's going on. Taking a power curve is a different story – steady-state running is not the way to do it on a rolling road.

For an acceleration run, you need a computer with software that captures the torque at a given sample rate, usually based on roller speed (mph). You drive against the roller in one gear, from low revs to maximum, and the computer records the load and speed, calculating the bhp from these numbers. This is not as simple as it sounds.

On the front of my machine I have three dials. These allow me to adjust the rollers for simulated load. I can dial in the weight of the vehicle, the power needed to overcome wind resistance (at 55mph) and the rolling resistance (again at 55mph). This allows me to accurately simulate road conditions for fuel consumption tests. If you think I go to all that trouble for a single power run you are sadly mistaken!

There are a lot of reasons why a rolling road is not as accurate as an engine dyno. One of them, which is often disregarded, is that the

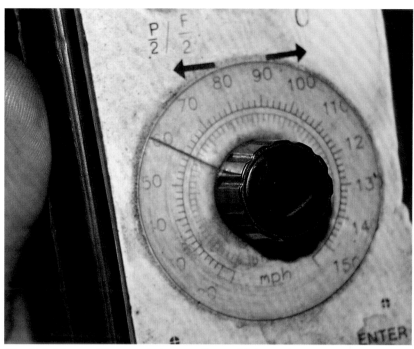

Fig. 5.4. Most rolling roads have rollers which can be set to rotate at a certain road-speed, in this case 60mph.

power of the engine is constantly changing. As combustion chambers heat up, power fades. As oil and coolant temperatures change, the power produced at the flywheel also changes. If you are involved in accurate research, you have to carefully monitor all these parameters. As a rolling-road operator, I simply keep an eye on coolant temperature and try to start my recording from the same coolant temperature each time.

The acceleration rate does have an effect on the final reading. If the engine accelerates too quickly you get a higher reading. This appears to be due to the inertia of the rollers coming into play. What I have done is to adjust the rolling road acceleration rate to give me a very close approximation to known cars. For example, I had a BMW showing 177bhp on an inertia roller. On my rollers I got exactly the same power figure from that same car, in both cases corrected for standard temperature and air pressure.

For cars producing between 130 and 200bhp this method seems to give realistic numbers, and it's

repeatable to within a bhp or two, given the limitations of the system and the changes in actual power between runs. For smaller engines, like a full-race 2CV, I have to increase the acceleration rate of the rollers, otherwise it would take all day to get to maximum rpm! On big 300bhp V8 engines maximum rpm rush up so fast you can't be sure it isn't wheel-spin. For these engines, I increase the roller load to slow everything down. I have to admit that there's an element of 'feel' to it. I've done over 5000 power runs now, and I think I can tell when it's all over too soon – or not.

What you get from all this is a power figure at the wheels across the rev range – totally meaningless! The rolling resistance of the tyres depends on road speed. If I run the car up in third gear the road speed reaches maybe 90mph. If I run it in fourth gear the rollers might reach 120 mph. In third I have less power loss through the wheels than I have in fourth gear, which means that in third (at for example, 6000rpm) I have 80bhp at the wheels. At

6000rpm in fourth I have only 70bhp at the wheels. That missing 10bhp is being lost due to the road wheels rotating at 120mph instead of 90mph.

The clever bit is measuring the rolling losses on the run down, and adding these to the 'at-the-wheels' figure. I can run in any gear and get the same power curve – but only after the rolling losses have been measured and added to the 'at-the-wheels' figure. If I look at the 'at-the-wheels' power in different gears at the same rpm I get a totally different reading.

To prove the point I ran a Golf GTI at 3000rpm, and recorded the power at the wheels. I then put another 10psi into the tyres. This higher tyre pressure reduces the amount of distortion of the side-wall, and hence reduces the rolling losses. I 'gained' nearly 5bhp at the wheels. Moral: if you want more power at the wheels, or improved fuel consumption, keep your tyres up to pressure. From this you can see that the idea of calculating a transmission loss which is common to all cars is patent nonsense – you need to know the road speed, the tyre size and its rolling resistance. If you get big variations at the wheels from week-on-week tests, then you may well have been very careless with your tyre pressures, or you have been changing the wheels.

From my experience the major loss is in the tyres. If I dip the clutch and keep the car in gear while I measure coast-down losses I get some added drag – possibly from the gear oil in the transmission, but more likely due to the clutch dragging plus the load on the release bearing. To state that you get a given percentage (often quoted as something like 15% or 25%) only shows a total ignorance of how the whole thing works. No shame in that. I used to happily measure power at the wheels and quote it – because I was ignorant of exactly what I was measuring. Ignorance isn't stupidity – it's just a case of not knowing what you are talking about.

Now that you have a good understanding of what you are measuring, and how you should go about it, you're in a better position to choose your rolling road and the operator who is going to map/set up your pride and joy.

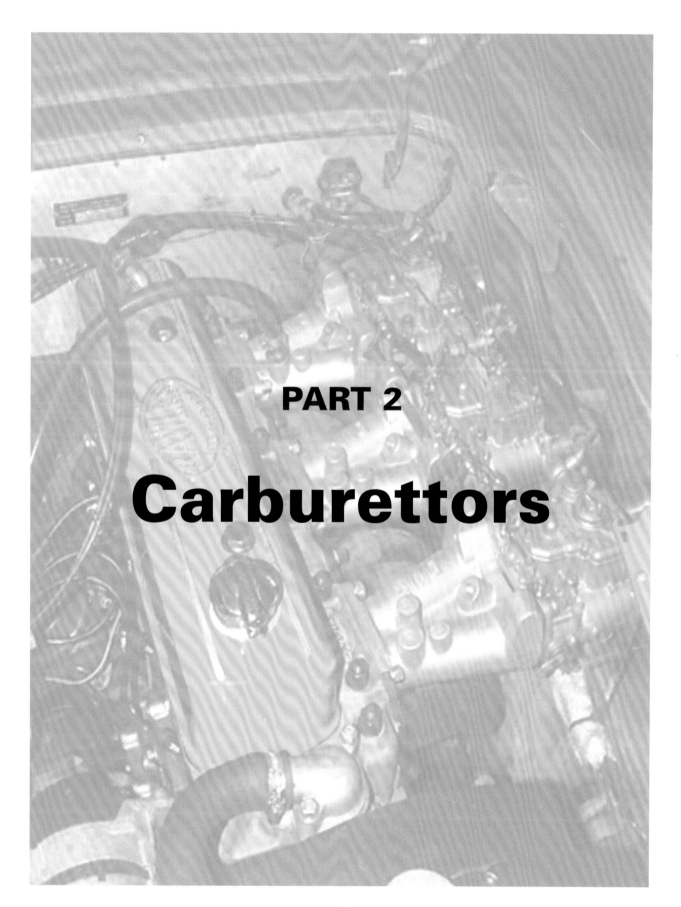

PART 2

Carburettors

Chapter 6

Carburettor theory

Introduction

Before you can adjust, set up, or modify anything it helps to have an understanding of how the thing works. This section covers the basics of carburation principles – based on a requirement for high specific power output.

Basic principles

To make the most basic of carburettors you simply connect an air tube to the inlet manifold and put a variable restrictor across the opening. The most common form of variable restrictor is a butterfly. This is simply a disc fitted to a spindle, and it's the most popular way of controlling the throttle on an engine.

We can arrange to throttle the engine in many different ways, but there are two popular systems in general use. Firstly, we can link all the intake ports to a single chamber, and then put our butterfly on the intake to the chamber. In this way a single butterfly controls all the cylinders, and this is the most common method for standard production engines.

However, for a competition engine there is a better way. We can have one butterfly for every cylinder, which means that each cylinder can have its own separate intake system. The less bends and twists in the intake, the less restrictions there are to the engine breathing.

Fig. 6.1. The gorgeous Maserati 300S sports-car six-cylinder engine uses a triple Weber carburettor set-up.

The butterfly, or throttle plate, can take different forms. The simplest, and most common, form is a disc mounted on a central spindle. When the butterfly plate is in line with the intake port, the only restriction to airflow is the spindle across the middle of the intake bore. An alternative is to use a slide, which pulls to one side and leaves the intake totally unrestricted. Slide throttles were all the fashion a while back for competition engines, but they can be very troublesome on road cars.

With high rpm and a closed throttle the engine is pulling hard on the throttle plate, trying to suck air past it. In resisting the flow, a lot of pressure is put upon the plate, which tends to pull it towards the engine. This loads the bearings, and on a slide-throttle system the slides tend to stick under this high vacuum. Slides are also more difficult to seal in the closed position. Roller bearings help the situation, but mechanically slide throttles are more difficult to manufacture, which is why circular butterflies, or near circular butterfly plates are much more popular. This is the system used on the Weber DCOE and Dellorto DHLA carburettors.

The dimensions of the intake system, in terms of both length and diameter, are very important to engine performance. The diameter

Fig. 6.2. A typical carburettor throttle butterfly. The cut-away sections of the butterfly expose the progression drillings earlier than normal.

is what dictates air speed within the intake system. To illustrate this, imagine blowing through a pea-shooter, or blow-pipe. If you swapped your 10mm diameter pea-shooter for a 100mm diameter drain pipe, how far could you shoot your peas, or blow your darts? Not very far! Inside the carburettor main bore you will find a restriction. This is called a 'venturi'. The job of the venturi is to speed up the air as it passes over the main jet.

With an engine we need a compromise between being too small on intake bore diameter, which might restrict breathing at high rpm and wide-open throttle, and too large, which means very

low air speed at low rpm and small throttle openings. A standard 2.0 litre engine might have all four cylinders breathing through a single venturi of 30mm diameter, but when we modify the engine we might need four individual venturis each of 36mm diameter. This sounds like a big increase in total area, but what a lot of people forget is that four cylinders pulling through one intake bore do not all demand air at the same time, but rather take their turn one after the other. There is a certain amount of overlap, but the overall restriction is not as bad as it might first appear. Up to a point, the bigger we go on butterfly diameter and venturi size, the better the top-end performance, and the more the low speed power suffers.

To all this airflow we somehow need to add the right amount of fuel. An engine is not like a bonfire, where the more fuel you add the better it goes. With competition engines we are working hard to get as much air into the engine as possible, along with the right amount of fuel, but there are limits, restrictions and compromises. Theoretically we need to add exactly the right amount of fuel to the available air so that all the fuel is burned with no excess air left over.

When we have this balance exactly right we call this mixture

Fig. 6.3. This cutaway of the carb venturi shows how the air speed increases as the air passes through the restriction.

Fig. 6.4. Weber DCOE venturis come in various sizes depending on the estimated power output. Always use the smallest that you can.

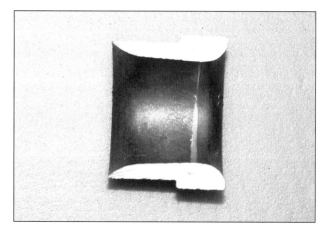

ratio of fuel and air 'chemically correct', or 'stoichiometric'. When we have excess air we call this a 'weak' mixture, and weak mixtures burn much hotter than we need, often causing parts of the engine to melt (like spark plugs or piston tops) – not a good idea!

If we have an excess of fuel for the available air, we call this a 'rich' mixture. Rich mixtures burn cooler, but we waste a lot of fuel, which just passes out through the exhaust pipe, often producing a sooty black smoke. Generally, engine tuners regard a richer mixture as being safe, but this isn't the whole story. If you run very rich mixtures for too long, the excess fuel finds its way inside the engine where it dilutes lubricating oil and washes lubricant off the cylinder walls. Rapid cylinder bore wear is the result.

For maximum power we need a slightly rich mixture – just a tiny amount of excess fuel to be sure that we use up every last particle of air that we worked so hard to get into the engine in the first place.

The next consideration for mixture ratios is not so much the ratio of fuel and air, but the way it is mixed together. This we call 'mixture presentation'. Engine designers go to great lengths to ensure that the fuel and air are mixed in such as way as to influence either power output, or fuel economy but you seldom get both together. As engine tuners we are looking for power, and this means making sure that the fuel is mixed as homogeneously as possible with the available air.

If there are lots of bends in the intake system, we find that the air turns the corners better than the fuel. The fuel, being heavier, tends to try and go straight on, banging into the port walls and sticking there, rather than staying in the airflow. This is another reason why straight ports work better than curved ones – even given the same airflow capacity.

If the air speed is high (smaller port diameters) the fuel gets swept

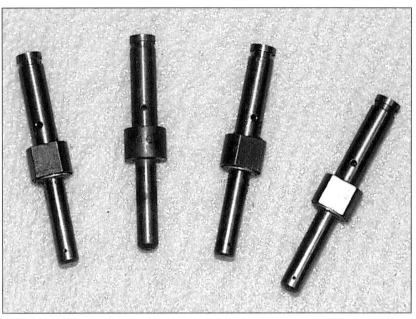

Fig. 6.5. Weber carb accelerator pump jets.

along and stays in suspension, mixed with the air. If the air speed is low, the fuel tends to lose momentum and drop out onto the floor of the port. 'Wet mixtures', where the fuel has dropped out or stuck to a port wall, leave lots of unburned fuel in the exhaust pipe (showing up as hydrocarbons on the gas analyser) which is a total waste of fuel, and also robs us of power.

At very high air speeds we have a different problem. The air is moving so fast that we can't get the fuel mixed with the air quickly enough, before it has passed through into the engine – there simply isn't enough time available. In this situation we can help matters by introducing the fuel as far away from the engine as possible. At very low air speeds we have the opposite problem. We need to introduce the fuel close up to the engine so that it doesn't drop out of the air stream. Nobody said it was easy!

Snap acceleration, or acceleration fuelling, overcomes a basic problem with fuel being heavier than air. When you open the throttle suddenly, the air can accelerate very quickly to meet engine demand, but the fuel does

not. In a carburettor, the fuel gets left behind and you have a very weak mixture reaching the engine, initially at least. This comes across as a big flat spot, felt as a sudden drop in power, which then comes back with a bang. To overcome this problem, most carburettors are fitted with a mechanical pump to deliver extra fuel when the throttle is suddenly snapped open.

To make changes on carburettors you need a large range of jets to cover starting, idle and maximum power.

Finally, we need to know about mixture ratio values, and what gives the best power. Sadly this isn't as simple as it might first appear. Theoretically we need just enough fuel mixed with the air to consume all the available air. This is a chemically correct mixture ratio given the rather fancy name 'stoichiometric'. You might also hear it called 'Lambda 1', a value assigned to an electrical sensor fitted into some exhaust systems for reading oxygen content, which relates to mixture ratio.

Stoichiometric fuel ratios are fine in theory, but if we want fuel economy we need to run with less fuel, and in this situation we actually want a weak mixture. A

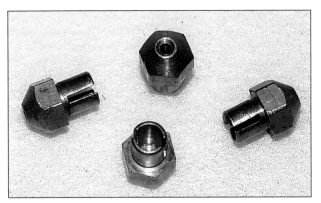

Fig. 6.6. Weber carb main jets.

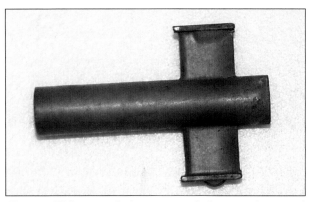

Fig. 6.7. This extended aux venturi changes the tuned length of the system to avoid unwanted pulses upsetting the fuel flow.

weaker mixture is okay for cruising on light throttle, but for maximum power we need a little excess fuel to make sure that all of the air is consumed. How much extra fuel will depend on the engine type, its manifold design, and many other external factors. The only way to arrive at the right mixture ratio for maximum power is to run the engine on an engine dyno or rolling road and measure the power output.

Basic carburettor fuelling

The butterfly controls the amount of air that can flow into the engine, regardless of the engine's demands. Next you put a fuel feed tube at 90° to the main airflow, and sit this in a little bowl of petrol. The level of the petrol is such that the fuel sits just below the surface of the petrol feed tube. As the throttle is opened, air moves through the bore of the air tube, and in doing so passes over the liquid petrol sitting in the petrol feed tube. The speed of the air causes some of the fuel at the surface to be picked up into the air steam. This is basically how a carburettor works.

The fuel is maintained at the right level by a float system, operating in a reservoir known as the float chamber. The fuel supply is also limited by a restriction, or what we call a 'jet'. The main restriction to flow is the main jet,

which can be changed to give us the right mixture ratio for the amount of air passing through the carburettor body.

In order to make things a little more efficient, we have a narrowed section of the air tube which we call a venturi, or 'choke'. This causes the air to speed up as it passes through the venturi and lift fuel from the jet more efficiently. As you can see, the speed of the air dictates how well the fuel is picked up. This relationship has a direct bearing on engine tuning for maximum power, and we call this relationship the fuel 'signal'.

Make the venturi smaller, and although we have good air speed (a strong signal), the size of the venturi acts as a restriction to airflow at full throttle and maximum rpm. Make the venturi larger, and air speed drops at lower rpm (producing a poor signal), which means fuel is not picked up efficiently, if at all!

Hence, when we fit carburettors we talk a lot about choke sizes. Big chokes produce good power at high rpm, but reduce tractability. It's a trade off all the time. The trick is to get the best compromise on choke size that matches the rest of the engine modifications.

There are tricks that can be employed in carburettor design to help matters. We can have a second venturi inside the first to speed up air locally over the fuel outlet. We call this an 'auxiliary

venturi' (aux venturi). It helps to pull fuel off at lower engine rpm until the motor really gets going. Both Weber and Dellorto race carburettors use aux vents.

Fuel is pulled from the float chamber according to the air speed passing over the main jet outlet. In the Weber/Dellorto carburettor a small aux venturi is fitted around this main jet outlet to increase air speed locally over the jet. The bore size of this aux venturi affects the way in which fuel delivery starts. Larger bore sizes bring the main circuit in later, smaller ones bring it in earlier.

Some carburettors fitted to certain engine models (Chrysler/Roots Holbay Hunter for example) come with an extended, very long, aux venturi. This is necessary to change the tuned length of the venturi, in order to overcome the problem of unwanted pulsing in the standard length aux venturi. This pulsing phenomenon can be used to our advantage – see the following section 'Pulse tuning theory'.

It is this question of matching the venturi size to the rest of the engine that leads to carburettors being available in different body sizes. A Weber 40DCOE or Dellorto 40DHLA has a body size of 40mm with a largest practical choke size of 32/33mm. You can also buy Webers or Dellortos with 45mm bodies, 48mm and even 50mm. Each has a range of choke sizes available which allows you to find the best possible match to your modified engine.

The key word here is match. Just because 50DCOEs/DHLAs have the best potential for maximum power, it doesn't mean they are going to be the optimum choice for your stock 1100cc engine. Your engine has to be able to pull enough air through that large venturi in order for it to work.

Pulse tuning theory

When air moves through a pipe it can produce a sound wave. This is how many musical instruments work – the trumpet for example. When an engine runs, it draws air through the carburettor, and in doing so creates a sound wave. This sound wave has energy which can be used to increase engine performance. The wave starts at the engine intake valve and moves towards the carburettor intake trumpet. On reaching the end of the trumpet (more commonly called a bell-mouth) this wave is reflected, changing sign and direction. The result is a positive pulse moving towards the engine. This pulse works like free supercharging, forcing air and fuel into the engine.

The overall length of the intake system from inlet valve to bell-mouth entry determines the engine rpm at which this positive pulse effect takes place. Unfortunately, there will also be an engine rpm where the effect is negative, with fuel and air being pushed *out* of the engine. This can often be seen on wide-open throttle as a fuel mist, blowing around the intake trumpets. This effect often leads to a rich mixture as the pulse returns back down the inlet, carrying much of the additional fuel with it. Effectively, the same air has passed the aux venturi twice, once going out, the second time coming back, pulling fuel off from the jet on each pass.

We need to find the best compromise on tract length that makes best use of the positive pulse, while putting the negative pulse at an rpm where the engine does not normally run. With the Weber and Dellorto carburettors we can tune the pulse length simply by changing the length of the intake trumpet. Some engine builders have a 'favourite' bell-mouth which they use on everything, but you must remember that it is the *overall length* of the inlet tract which determines the pulse effect. Use a shorter, or longer, inlet manifold and the overall length changes, altering the tuned length of the system.

In order to maximize the pulse tuning effect you need to keep changes in section to a minimum. Stepping up from a small bore inlet manifold to a large bore carburettor, for example, should be avoided. This is another good reason for not selecting too large a carburettor.

Carburettor operation

Idle stage

The operation of Weber or Dellorto side-draught carburettors can be broken down into three main areas; idle, progression and main fuelling. Starting with the idle, this is the easiest area to get right, but each area overlaps the other, and incorrect tuning at one stage can make it impossible to get the next stage right.

The idle mixture is controlled by an adjusting screw, and within reasonable limits you can achieve the right idle mixture using a fairly wide range of idle-jet sizes. Idle speed is controlled by the butterfly stop, and with this set to the required engine idle rpm, only the idle drilling is exposed to engine vacuum. Fuel is drawn from the float chamber through the idle jet, where it mixes with air from the side-drilling in the idle jet on Weber carburettors, or through side drillings in the idle-jet holder on Dellortos. This emulsified mixture of fuel and air is then drawn into the engine after passing by the tapered idle mixture screw.

Fig. 6.8. The overall length of the induction system will dictate how and when the pulses add, or subtract, to the power.

Turning the idle mixture screw out allows more fuel to enter the engine and therefore richens the mixture. Turning the screw in reduces the amount of fuel and weakens the mixture. Take care when screwing the idle mixture screw in. If you reach the limit (the screw simply bottoms out) and then over-tighten the screw, you can break the body of the carburettor casting, or damage the fine taper of the screw.

As a starting point, you should gently bottom out each screw and then turn each one out the same number of turns. One-and-a-half to two complete revolutions out is a good base setting. With the engine at idle, you can then adjust each screw to give the required mixture. You can determine this with the aid of a CO meter, or you can simply

Fig. 6.9. Idle mixture screw (arrowed). There is no 'ideal' setting but it should end up about 3.5 turns out, depending on the idle jet size.

Fig. 6.10. Weber DCOE carburettor idling and progression phases.

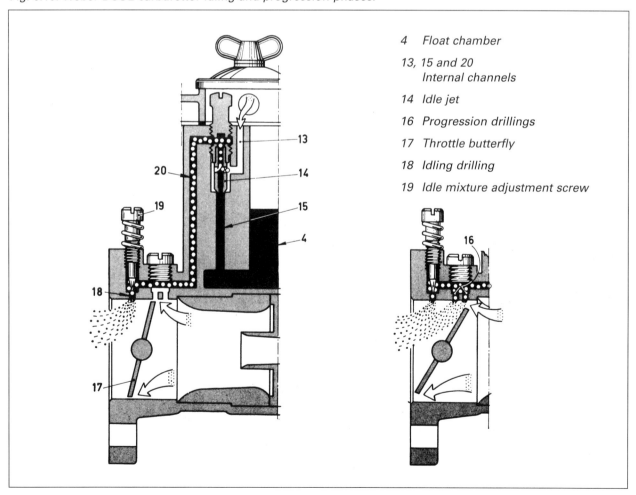

4   Float chamber
13, 15 and 20 Internal channels
14   Idle jet
16   Progression drillings
17   Throttle butterfly
18   Idling drilling
19   Idle mixture adjustment screw

Fig. 6.11. These are progression drillings. They feed fuel into the engine until the throttle is open enough for the main jets to work.

adjust the mixture to give the most even running. On highly tuned engines you may find that the idle is very lumpy and requires a relatively rich idle mixture, possibly 3–5% CO.

Idle speed should not be too low if high-lift camshafts have been installed. The cams suffer maximum stress at low engine rpm. 1200rpm or more may be needed to achieve a stable idle.

Progression stage

As the throttle opens, the air speed inside the carburettor increases, but initially this is not high enough to bring the main jet into operation. The progression drillings supply fuel on initial opening of the butterfly to 'fill in' the gap between idle and main-jet operation.

The progression drillings are supplied with fuel from the passage that also feeds the idle system. As the butterfly opens, one drilling at a time is uncovered, and fuel starts to be drawn into the engine. By the time the last drilling is supplying fuel, the main jet operation should be well under way, and the idle and progression circuits then become redundant – there isn't sufficient vacuum

present to pull much fuel from the tiny drillings.

Main-jet operation

Air passing through the auxiliary venturi moves fast enough to create a partial vacuum that pulls fuel from the main-jet system. Fuel is drawn from the main float chamber, via the main jet, which is fitted into the bottom of the emulsion tube. At the same time, the vacuum also pulls air

into the system from the air-corrector jet located at the top of the emulsion tube. Drillings in the emulsion tube then dictate exactly how this air and fuel are mixed together before delivery to the outlet in the centre of the aux venturi.

The main jet limits the amount of fuel that can be drawn off for any given signal strength (level of vacuum present). To richen the overall mixture, you increase the main jet size; to weaken the mixture you select a smaller main jet.

The air-corrector jet works in the same manner, but by restricting the amount of air available to the emulsion tube. By pre-mixing the fuel and air, an emulsion is presented at the main-jet outlet point, rather than raw fuel which may not mix well with the main air stream at lower air speeds (low revs, small throttle opening). The air-corrector jet tends to have more effect at higher rpm. Reducing the air-corrector jet size will richen the mixture more at high rpm than at low rpm. By increasing the air-corrector jet size you weaken top-end fuelling more than at the bottom end. We call this 'tipping the fuel slope', because it alters the way in which the main jet supplies fuel across the rpm range.

The emulsion tube is the mixing

Fig. 6.12. A selection of main jets. The main jet system supplied the bulk of the fuel for maximum power.

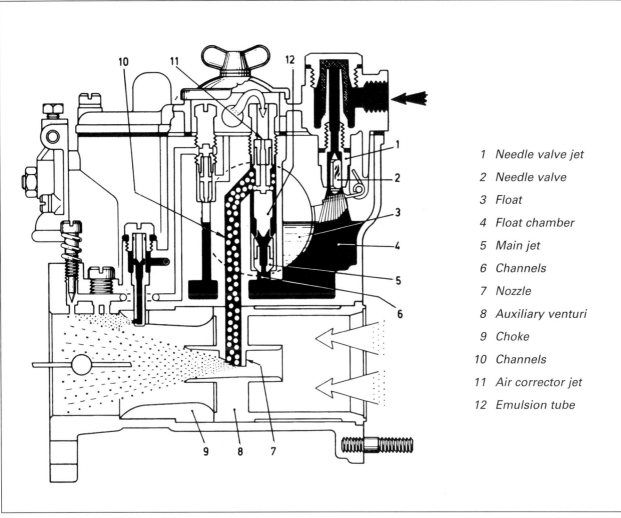

1   Needle valve jet

2   Needle valve

3   Float

4   Float chamber

5   Main jet

6   Channels

7   Nozzle

8   Auxiliary venturi

9   Choke

10 Channels

11 Air corrector jet

12 Emulsion tube

Fig. 6.13. Weber DCOE carburettor main-jet operation

Fig. 6.14. A selection of air corrector jets. Air correctors tip the fuel slope. A bigger air corrector means weaker top end mixture and vice versa.

Fig. 6.15. Ideally the air correctors (1) should be at least a couple of sizes larger than the main jets (2).

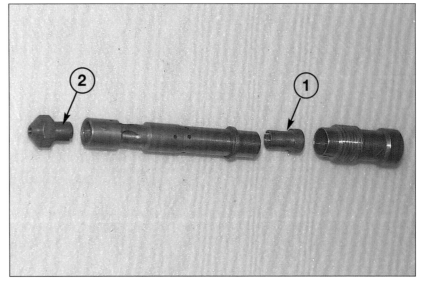

Fig. 6.16. A selection of emulsion tubes. The emulsion tube influences the mid-rpm fuelling and can be checked by comparing power curves.

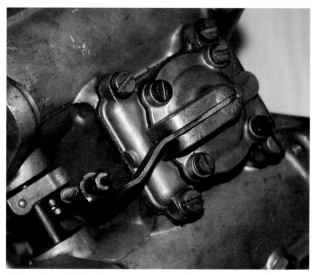

Fig. 6.17. Dellorto carbs use a diaphragm accelerator pump, which is said to be more accurate and consistent than a Weber piston pump.

chamber, and the shape, size and position of the drillings in the tube dictate how the emulsion is pre-mixed. This has a big influence on mid-rpm-range fuelling and mixture presentation.

Emulsion tubes

So much has been written about emulsion tubes and Weber carburettors, yet all of the published material that I could find left me totally confused. 'Ask around' seemed to be the best advice available.

Having played with emulsion tubes and looked at how they really work, I've found that it isn't that complicated at all. Basically, the emulsion tube is a mixing chamber. Fuel comes in one end via the main jet, and air comes in the other end via the air-corrector jet. The thing to note is that the *fuel* comes to the main outlet in the venturi from around the *outside* of the emulsion tube. The *air* comes from *inside* the tube.

Think of this as a simple 'T'-junction. Air comes from one side of the 'T', fuel from the other, with the outlet in the middle. You can juggle the amount of air and fuel going into the engine by altering the jets at either end.

When the engine isn't running,

the float level dictates the level at which the fuel sits in the emulsion tube. As you begin to use fuel, the main jet becomes a restriction, and the level of fuel around the outside of the tube drops. This uncovers any air holes in the lower part of the emulsion tube that were previously below the fuel level. Uncovering the lower holes bleeds in more air, which weakens the mixture. Adding air at this stage also helps to mix the fuel and air together, although this isn't a true mixing but an 'emulsion' of fuel and air – hence the term 'emulsion tube'.

This feature of the emulsion tube is essential to overcome the carburettor's main problem – that of running richer mixtures at high engine rpm. At low air speeds the vacuum signal is low, and fuel is pulled from the main-jet outlet very inefficiently. As the air speed increases, the fuel flow gathers momentum, and fuel flow relative to airflow increases, making the mixture richer. The air-bleed holes in the emulsion tube are there in order to counteract this natural high-speed richness.

We have already noted that the fuel is drawn from around the outside of the emulsion tube. By altering the thickness of the emulsion tube, you can alter the

volume of fuel available on initial throttle operation. A thinner tube allows a richer mixture as the main system takes over from the progression drillings. A thicker tube reduces the initial mixture strength. Once the main system is under way, the thickness of the tube makes little difference to the fuelling.

Acceleration fuelling

As fuel is heavier than air, we can have a problem on a carburettor with very sudden snap throttle opening. Snap the throttle open from low speed, and the air moves into the engine very rapidly – too fast for the fuel to react and keep the mixture constant. The result is a weak mixture which we call a 'flat spot'. The engine gulps and can, in extreme cases, cut out altogether.

In this situation we can't rely on vacuum alone to move the fuel, it has to be assisted mechanically. This is done with a pump, known as the accelerator pump, or accel pump for short. On Weber carbs, the accel pump is a small piston fitted in a bore which is filled with fuel from the main float chamber. A mechanical linkage presses on a spring, which in turn moves the piston. By using a spring to operate the piston, the mechanical linkage can move directly with the throttle linkage, to full open from idle if necessary, on snap throttle opening. The spring then operates the piston over a given time period, depending on the strength of the spring and the size of the bleed-back valve.

The bleed-back valve is a small valve in the base of the float chamber that supplies the fuel to the accel pump. This allows fuel to bleed back into the float chamber when the accel-pump piston is moving slowly. Rapid accel-pump piston movement closes the valve and allows most of the fuel to be forced out of the accel-pump jet, with a small amount bleeding back depending on the size of the calibration hole in the jet. By varying the size of this calibration hole, you can alter the total amount of fuel injected by the accel-pump piston.

The accel-pump jet is the final restriction to fuel delivery from the accel pump. This jet directs fuel into the engine in line with the airflow. Due to the nature of the design, fuel can also be drawn from this jet at high rpm/air speed, so the accel-pump jet can influence the flat-out fuel mixture setting.

On Dellorto carbs, a diaphragm rather than a piston is used to pump the fuel, but the end result is the same.

Choke operation

On DCOE/DHLA carbs you have a rich mixture supply system for cold starting. This operates independently of the main carb circuits. When you operate the choke lever, two small pistons are lifted off their seats to allow fuel and air mixture to enter the engine. The higher you lift the pistons, the more fuel they add. Jetting for cold starting is not an exact science, and the jets supplied are usually always rich enough to get the job done. The larger competition carbs do not have cold start systems. To start the engine you simply operate the throttle rapidly several times to inject fuel from the accel-pump jets. Very few people bother to connect the cold start system, preferring to use the accel pump for cold starting.

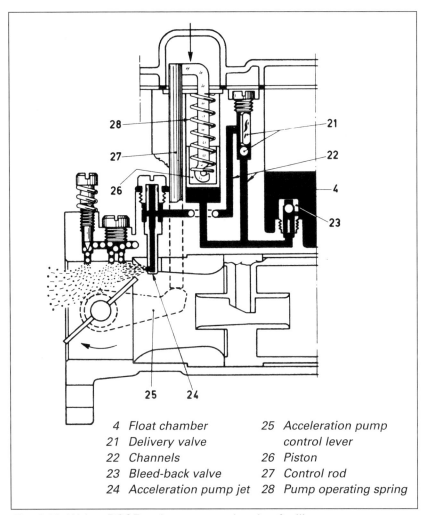

4	Float chamber	25	Acceleration pump
21	Delivery valve		control lever
22	Channels	26	Piston
23	Bleed-back valve	27	Control rod
24	Acceleration pump jet	28	Pump operating spring

Fig. 6.18. Weber DCOE carburettor acceleration fuelling.

Fig. 6.19. A Weber carb choke linkage. Most people don't bother with carb chokes; two or three pumps of the accel jets normally starts most race engines.

Chapter 7
Carburettor selection

How to choose the correct carburettor

When buying side-draught carburettors the temptation is always to select too large a carburettor for the engine's needs. Many professional engine builders inflate their power figures, either intentionally or through inaccurate customer feed-back, and this often leads to unrealistic expectations of power output. As a guide, 100bhp per litre is not an 'average' figure, for a two-valve-per-cylinder engine, it is often difficult to achieve. For a fast road engine, work on 60bhp-per-litre, and only consider 100bhp-per-litre for race engines. Four-valve-per-cylinder engines can produce 75bhp-per-litre in sensible fast road specification, and 140bhp-per-litre in full-race guise. These are guidelines only, but they are achievable if you put in the effort.

The following is an approximation of required choke size for power output – per cylinder. Multiply by the number of cylinders to get the total engine power output.

Carburettor selection starts with choke size requirement. There is little point in picking a 45DCOE carburettor if the power output of the engine demands nothing larger than a 32mm choke. Make sure that your required choke size is available for the carburettor you buy. Some engine builders will turn out chokes on the lathe to increase the bore size. If you exceed the largest choke size available for that carburettor, not only do you lose the original venturi shape, but you gain nothing in terms of airflow.

A classic example is the 40DCOE. This has a supplied factory choke size of 32/33mm. If you bore out the choke to 34mm, you gain nothing in terms of airflow through the carburettor. Once a choke size of 32mm has been exceeded, the flow restriction across the bore diameter of the carburettor is the auxiliary venturi. By turning out to 34mm you reduce air speed and hence signal strength over the main jet. *Don't do it!*

Fig. 7.1. Choke diameter selection chart.

For 4-stroke engines with one carburettor barrel per engine cylinder. The three curves correspond to maximum output engine speeds of 6000, 8000 and 10,000rpm.

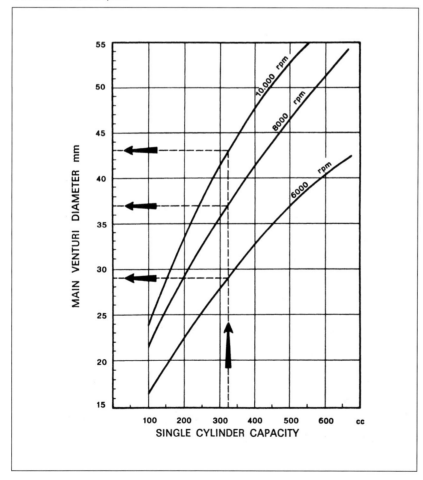

Chapter 8

Component installation

Carburettor installation

Fitting DCOE/DHLA carbs is not a complex operation – but you *must* get it right. The first mistake I see over and over again is the bolting of the carbs to the manifold. The nuts should not be bolted up tight. The carb should be fitted with either 'Thackery' washers, which act like springs, or rubber washers which do the same job. Only very old set-ups still use Thackery washers, the rubber washer with a cupped flat washer either side is the current mounting method. Retaining nuts must be of the locking type, and the carb must be free to flex on the mounts. If using Thackery washers, only tighten the nuts up until you can get a 0.025in (0.6mm) feeler blade between the coils of the washer. With rubber mounts, just tighten until the rubber is compressed but not squeezed out of the side of the cupped washers.

This flexible mounting is important, and is designed to

Above: Fig. 8.1. Thackery washers allow carbs to vibrate, but the springs are prone to breaking.

Left: Fig. 8.2. The rubber washer with mounting 'cups', as shown here, is the preferred method of carb mounting. Carbs should never be bolted solid to the manifold.

Below Left: Fig. 8.3. Mounting the carbs using twin O-ring seals with a plastic centre is asking for trouble.

Below: Fig. 8.4. A single O-ring in a 'Misab' plate is the best way of sealing carbs to the manifold.

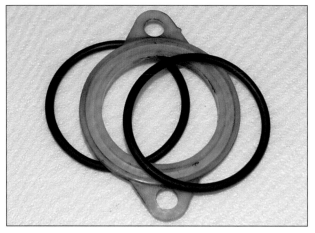

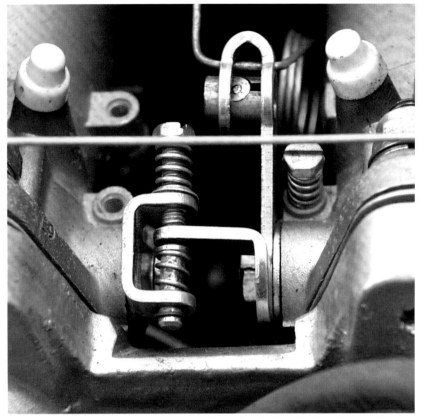

Fig. 8.5. A decent finger-and-yoke linkage is vital for balancing carbs correctly and accurately. Poor linkages are a nightmare.

isolate the carb from engine vibration. This vibration upsets the float level and can cause misfiring at high rpm.

The carb seals against the manifold face with rubber O-rings. There are two types generally in use, one good, one useless. If you have a plastic centre to the seal arrangement, with an O-ring either side, throw it away! The type you want is a single aluminium plate with a single rubber O-ring bonded to it. This is commonly known as a 'Misab' plate.

The double O-ring seals work okay until you get a spit-back in the carb, or perhaps find the wrong gear and force the engine rpm very high on the overrun (throttle closed). With a spit-back, the O-ring will pop out of the groove and create an air leak. With a high rpm overrun situation, the seal gets sucked into the manifold by the very high manifold vacuum. Either way you have to unbolt the carbs in order to re-fit the seal every time it happens.

I have seen these double seals

Fig. 8.6. Weber DCOE linked throttle linkage on twin-carb set-up.

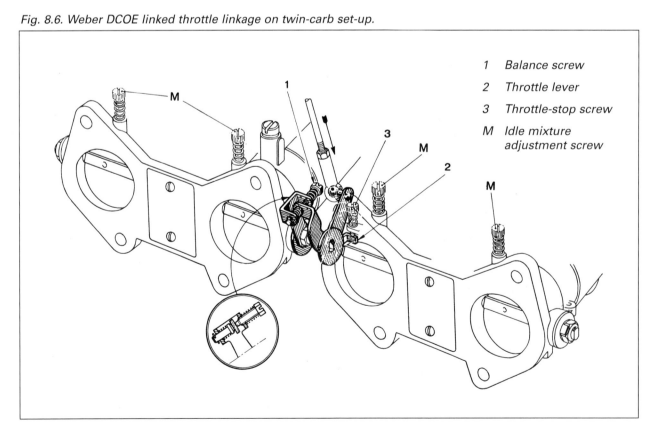

1 Balance screw

2 Throttle lever

3 Throttle-stop screw

M Idle mixture adjustment screw

Fig. 8.7. Return springs should be fitted so as to avoid inducing any twist in the carb spindle.

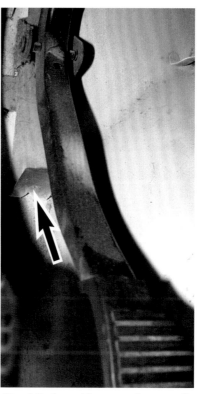

Fig. 8.8. A positive stop (arrowed) on the throttle pedal saves a lot of drama due to over-stretched cables and stressed linkages.

super-glued in place, but they seldom hold. The single O-ring plate just allows air pressure past in either direction, and you never have a problem with them. Why use anything else?

The next biggest headache is the throttle linkage. Weber and Dellorto carbs use an excellent finger-and-yoke link between a pair of carbs, but you only need one throttle stop for idle speed control. There are left and right-hand lugs on most carbs, but you don't need both of them. The master carb is the one fitted with the finger link, and this has the throttle-stop screw. The slave carb has the yoke, and this should not have any throttle stop at all.

If you get it wrong and put the throttle stop on the slave carb you will have nightmares chasing the balance and idle speed, two throttle stops will cause even more confusion!

The linkage to the throttle pedal fits onto the master carb, and you should check for obstructions throughout the linkage's range of movement. Hoses, cable-ties, even return springs can be trapped as the throttle opens. The better design of linkage has a non-linear opening rate. Initial throttle pedal travel gives a slow opening for good slow-speed control. As you approach the fully-open throttle position, the action speeds up. This is done using linkage angles or cam cable wheels. Return springs can also cause big problems in carb setting up. *Do not* put return springs on the far ends of the carb spindles. All this does is twist the spindle, because the other end is fixed by the idle stop position. The twisting of the spindle puts the carbs out of balance, and no amount of adjustment will put it right.

Return springs should act against the main linkage, pulling the operating lever back to the stop. The internal springs in the carbs will keep the butterflies in sync. You should make the obvious check for full throttle opening, but also check that you have a functioning throttle pedal stop. On full throttle you do not want to be putting any undue strain on the throttle cable. Most throttle cable breaks are due to not having a proper throttle stop on the pedal. In the workshop this may not look like much of a problem, but when the driver is constantly stamping the pedal to the floor, the cable either stretches, pulls out, or breaks.

Always check the fitted angle of the carbs. You can mount side-draught carbs at a down-draught angle, but there is a limit. The float chamber will not find the right level for the jets if you tip the carb up too far. Five degrees is the recommended maximum. Don't think that just because you've bought a purpose-made inlet manifold you can't have a problem. Some manifolds exceed this angle considerably and never work properly. Also remember that the installed angle of the engine may not be standard, so this must also be taken into account.

Fig. 8.9. The carbs cannot be mounted at too high an angle, or the floats will spill fuel when stationary, and flood at high speed. With this manifold the carbs are mounted at the same angle as the manifold mating face on the cylinder head.

Fig. 8.10. A little lock wire on Weber carb tops saves you losing them. They are prone to vibrating loose on some engines.

Finally, on Weber carbs, it's well worth securing the screw-fitting carb tops using a little lock wire, as they are prone to vibrating loose on some engines.

Fig. 8.11. The S-bend in the inlet manifold works a lot better than you would think from just looking at it (see text).

Manifold selection

This is fairly straightforward, since there generally isn't a vast range of choice for most engine applications. In most cases the manifold will have been designed to allow the carbs to fit inside the engine bay without hitting the bulkhead, front panel or inner wing. Don't be too concerned about the bends in the manifold. In some cases, an S-bend can be an advantage in getting a longer tract length in a confined space. Flow-bench tests that I have carried out on S-bend manifolds show very small losses in maximum flow over a straight tube in most instances. However, there is one point to note.

If the angle at the carb joining face is even moderately down-draught, you may well get maximum airflow at less than full throttle. This is because the butterfly sitting at an angle can

Fig. 8.12. Not getting full throttle? On some set-ups less than 100% throttle gives the best power!

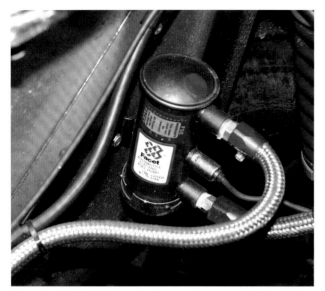

Fig. 8.13. A high-flow fuel pump is essential for high-powered engines. Electric pumps for carbs usually supply about 8psi.

Fig. 8.14. A pressure regulator will drop the supplied pressure down to about 3 to 3.5psi to avoid overcoming the resistance of the float needle.

redirect the airflow down into the manifold. Opening the butterfly to full throttle can often reduce the maximum airflow through the manifold system.

You sometimes feel this on the rolling road when, as you lift off the power increases slightly. Many operators put this down to their imagination, but it really can be that you get more power on less than full throttle – a point well worth checking. Adjusting the linkage can sometimes give more power at full throttle.

Fuel pump selection

You can encounter nightmare situations in setting up carbs that have nothing to do with the carburettors at all. Fuel supply is critical, and you can get it wrong in

either direction – too much, or too little. The obvious mistake is to modify the engine using big carbs, and then to use the standard mechanical fuel pump which came with the engine. This is never going to be up to the job, unless your engine simply isn't producing the power.

A classic example is the Ford Pinto engine. You can get this engine up to 145/150bhp on the stock fuel pump, but after that you *will* get power drop-off due to fuel starvation. The opposite end of the scale is to fit a massive electric pump delivering 8–10psi at the carb. This causes flooding on idle, and too high a float level at other times as the pressure overcomes the float needle seal.

Ideally you need a good pump with a pressure regulator fitted between the carb and the pump.

An adjustable regulator combined with a fuel filter gets the job done and isn't expensive. As far as fuel pump capacity goes, the calculation is simple. For every one bhp, you need a half-pint of fuel flow per hour as a theoretical *minimum*. To allow some safety margin, aim for at least 0.34 pints/bhp/hour. If you are metric, this equates to approximately one litre/bhp/hour. (Note: UK and European units of measurement, not USA.)

Feed this fuel to the pressure regulator and set the regulator to between 2 and 4psi. Aim for as much pressure as the system will stand without flooding the carbs on idle. I start with 3.5psi on my own engines. It sounds obvious, but make sure that the fuel lines are clear, and large enough to handle the required flow.

Chapter 9

Carburettor tuning

Introduction

There is no point at all in trying to tune a defective carburettor. All the jets, drillings and airways must be clear – obvious advice but so many people buy second-hand carbs that may have sat around for years gently corroding away inside. At least get them checked, if not rebuilt, before you try to tune them.

Next, set the float height at the right setting for your carbs. This is important for the overall performance on the road or track, since float height can play an important role during cornering and braking, as the fuel moves around inside the carb.

Also take a good look at the float needle and seat. Don't just check for sealing, you need to have a float-needle jet large enough to pass sufficient fuel for maximum power. The following guide shows which jets you need for various

power outputs – be realistic in your expectations and don't fit an overly large jet without good reason. The following chart indicates the needle valve sizes where one needle valve is fitted; where there is more than one needle valve (eg, with twin DCOEs) the maximum power for the engine should be divided by the number of needle valves to calculate the size for each valve:

Power (hp)	Needle valve jet size (mm)
Up to 60	1.50
61 to 110	1.75
111 to 150	2.00
151 to 180	2.25
181 to 200	2.50
Over 200	3.00
Alcohol fuel	3.00

Fig. 9.2. A basic compression check before you start any tuning isn't a bad idea.

The most important investment that you can put into tuning your carburettors, is time. It takes a long time to get everything right, but if you take the time, and work methodically, you will be rewarded with a sweet, responsive, engine that is a joy to drive. Rush the job and you'll have dead spots, flat spots and spit-backs – possibly with the added excitement of an under-bonnet fire!

I always make a cylinder compression check before I start any tuning. This will tell me if the engine is basically sound – or not. A check on tappet clearances isn't a bad idea either. So many people spend a lot of time trying to set up an engine that is never going to run right, no matter how expert the tuner is with carburettors.

Fig. 9.1. The float needle and seat must have enough flow for the engine's power output. Too small a seat will kill the power at speed.

Getting started

One of the most common questions you see in magazines' technical pages is about jet selection. People want to know what jets to fit into their carbs for a given engine. It really doesn't work like that. No two engines will use identical exhausts, inlet manifolds, compression ratios or any number of other parameters that affect carburation. A good starting point is to run whatever jets came with the carb – since you have to start somewhere, why buy more jets that you might not eventually need?

However, what you do need to do is pull the jets out and make a note of the sizes. As long as you have selected a carb size that is suitable for your engine, you should have jet sizing close enough to at least start the engine. If you bought carbs and changed the choke sizes straight away, try a main jet that is 4 x choke diameter as a starting point.

Start the engine and allow it to reach working temperature. This means that the thermostat is open, or you have at least 70°C on your gauge. If an electric fan is fitted you know the engine is really hot when this cuts in and out on idle.

Idle adjustment

Set the idle-stop screw to a point where the engine will idle anywhere between 1000rpm and 1300rpm. If the engine keeps spitting back through the carbs, turn the mixture adjusters out until it stops. The spitting back is caused by weak mixture still burning in the combustion chamber when the inlet valve opens. Turning the screws out richens the mixture and cures the spit-back. Next try moving the adjusters in, and then out, until you have an engine that will at least idle after a fashion. Check the ignition timing on idle.

Ignition timing has a lot to do with setting up carburettors and can be a useful tool in matching carbs to an engine for clean

progression – but more of this later, for now just check that you have an at idle ignition timing setting of around 8 to 10° BTDC.

In all probability, the engine will be shaking like a jelly on a plate. This is almost always due to carbs being out of balance. You can buy fancy push-in balancing gauges and vacuum gauges for setting carb balance, but all I ever use is a length of half-inch heater hose. Put one end of the hose to your ear and place the other end against the carb intake – listen to the hiss. Now compare the intake hiss between the master carb and the slave. The difference will be very obvious if the carbs are out of balance. Adjust the balance screw until you get the same intake hiss on both carbs.

You can check all four intakes for balance, but on early carbs you can't adjust for balance between chokes on the same carb. If this is out it's normally a twist in the spindle (check those return springs) or a faulty cylinder. Later SP Webers have a bypass screw which can be used to even out any imbalance – I recommend you leave these fully closed for the time being.

Now go back to the idle-mixture screws and re-adjust. Use a CO meter, Lambda reader or simply set the screws to the highest rpm/smoothest setting where the

Fig. 9.3. The position of the progression holes should be such that they are uncovered just as the butterfly moves off idle.

engine seems happy. As you correct the mixture, the engine rpm may need adjusting to maintain the required idle speed.

It may be that you cannot get a smooth idle, and the rpm is either too high or the engine dies when you try to slow it down. Check the position of the butterfly relative to the progression drillings. Remove the plugs above the progression holes, and use a torch to determine the position of the butterfly edge. If one or more holes are already uncovered, or even partially uncovered, then the butterfly needs to be further closed at the required idle rpm.

If your carburettors are the later Weber 'SP' type you can use the idle-bypass screws to bleed air past the butterfly. This will mean

Fig. 9.4. The idle bypass screws allow you to position the butterfly on idle relative to the progression drillings.

that you need to close down the throttle stop to return the idle rpm to normal. Open the bypass screws just enough to allow the throttle plate to close off the progression drillings and take them out of the idle equation.

On earlier carbs you can try a couple of tricks to achieve the same thing. The easiest way to close down the throttle without losing idle speed is to advance the ignition timing on idle. This will speed up the engine, and then you can return to normal idle rpm by closing the throttle. With engine management fitted to the engine you can do this very simply by tapping the keyboard to the optimum setting and saving the timing into the map.

With timing control by advance weights, you will have to turn the distributor to advance the timing, and then modify the full advance stops to limit maximum advance to the optimum setting. More on this later.

The second way of closing down the throttle without losing idle rpm is to drill a small hole in the butterfly to act as a bypass. This means taking the carbs off the engine for drilling, but it does work. Keep the holes somewhere between 0.8mm and 1.3mm

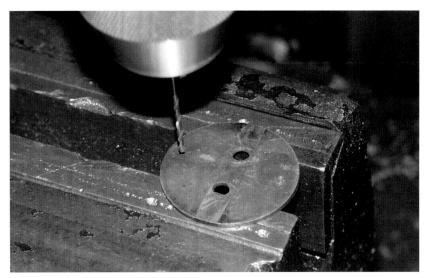

Fig. 9.5. If you have no bypass screws, you can drill a small hole in the butterfly to act as a bypass.

diameter. The bigger the hole, the greater the speed increase. If you go too far, you can always solder up the hole – the butterflies are brass and solder very nicely.

Remember that your aim is to have the progression holes just fully on the atmosphere side of the butterfly at your optimum idle speed. They should uncover just as you open the throttle from the idle position. If the situation is reversed, and the progression drillings are too far away from the edge of the butterfly, you will get a weak

mixture flat spot. In this case, your first option is to retard the ignition timing. Retarding the timing slows the engine, and you then have to recover the lost idle speed by opening the throttle stop. Always remember that when you move the ignition timing on idle, you will have to sort out the maximum advance afterwards unless you have engine management. This may mean bending advance weight stops, or opening them up depending on which way you move the idle timing.

Fig. 9.6. Many Dellorto carbs have the back edge of the butterfly cut away in the area of the progression drillings as standard . . .

Fig. 9.7 . . . which means that the progression holes come into play as soon as you open the throttle from idle.

Another way of bringing in the progression drillings earlier is to cut away the back edge of the butterfly in the area of the drillings. On Dellorto carbs, often this is done as standard. Thinning the butterfly exposes the drillings to engine vacuum a little sooner.

Progression

In all the published material that I've seen over the years, very little has been written about progression. Progression is the least understood aspect of carb tuning, yet it is the single most important factor in achieving a crisp, clean running, engine with smooth pick-up.

With the engine on idle, slowly open the throttle and let the revs rise. If the engine runs cleanly and sounds sharp, try opening the throttle a little further. What you want to do is make the engine run on the progression drillings at different rpm, the amount you open the throttle will achieve this. If this initial check proves okay you can forget progression until the road test stage. However, it's often the case that the engine coughs and spits-back or stumbles at some point.

What you need to do next is fix the throttle at the point where the misfire occurs. I use the throttle stop and wind it down until the engine starts to misbehave. You may have to remove any tension spring on the idle adjuster screw to gain additional movement if the spring becomes coil bound before the engine misfires.

At the misfire point, stop the engine. Now remove the plug above the progression drillings and check the position of the butterfly. As before, if you use a torch and move the throttle by hand you can see the edge of the butterfly. This will tell you whether the progression drillings are being uncovered by the butterfly at this point, or not. If they are, and the engine runs weak, the progression drillings are in the right place, but

the fuel supply to them is too weak. If the drillings are not being uncovered, then the butterfly is too far away on idle (see previous information on butterfly idle position in *'Idle adjustment'*). It may be necessary to put in an extra drilling closer to the butterfly, but this is a last resort since drilling the carb body is a one-way street.

It is possible to file, or machine, the edge of the butterfly around the drillings on the engine side so that the holes are exposed to engine vacuum earlier, as already detailed. All these tricks can be employed to position the drillings correctly relative to the idle position.

Using a CO meter, Lambda reader or sensitive ear, check the mixture condition once the progression drillings have been uncovered. If the mixture is weak, you can change the idle jet for a larger one. It is the idle jet that controls the mixture to the progression drillings. If you change the jet to richen progression mixture, don't forget that you will have to re-set the idle mixture screws, since the one jet feeds both systems.

The idle jet also has an air bleed, which alters the mixture overall, but more so on the progression drillings. To make life more complicated, there is no logic to the Weber numbering system. The idle jet settings get progressively richer in the following sequence:

F3, F1, F7, F5, F4, F2, F13, F11, F8, F9, F12, F6

With Dellorto carbs we have the luxury of sensible numbering, plus the ability to alter the air bleed without changing the idle fuel jet. On Dellortos the idle-air-bleed drillings are in the jet holder, not the jet. This means you can retain the same jet but change the holder to alter the air-bleed size.

Main fuelling operation

The main jet has more influence over the mixture than anything else on the carb. It dictates the

maximum fuel flow available at wide-open throttle, and hence the overall fuel/air mixture ratio. Please note that the main jet operates mainly on wide-open throttle. On idle you can remove the main jet/emulsion tube/air corrector complete assembly, and the engine will continue to tick over as before.

When selecting a main jet for an unknown engine, I always begin by revving the engine and just listening to the intake. If it cuts and splutters, fit a larger main jet, if it black smokes, fit a smaller jet. Then I like to take a 'snap-shot' of the mixture at about half-way up the rpm operating range. If the engine is thought to peak at 7000rpm, then I adjust the rolling road to hold the rpm at 3500rpm. Using a lambda mixture reader you can do this on the road. Hold the engine at the required rpm and then press the throttle to the floor. Don't snap the throttle open suddenly, because you will bring in the accel pump jets and the mixture will show rich. Select a high gear to keep the rpm acceleration rate down to a minimum.

On full throttle, check the lambda mixture reading. As a guide, if the main jet is way too small, you will get an engine cut as the throttle is opened wide. If it is far too large you will get a bad engine stutter with black smoke from the exhaust. Only when the mixture is somewhere near right will you get an accurate reading from the lambda mixture reader.

On a rolling road you can use a gas analyser to check the mixture. What you don't want to do is hold the engine on full throttle while the analyser takes its sample, which can take up to 15 seconds. This might be long enough to damage the engine if the mixture is far enough out. Holding the rpm at 3500, press the pedal to full throttle and wait five seconds. Next, quickly depress the clutch and pump the accelerator pedal several times. By pumping the throttle you will operate the accel pump system, which puts a lot of raw fuel through the engine. This will show up on the gas analyser as a very high hydrocarbon (HC) reading, and you can use this high HC reading as a marker. You watch the CO, and when the HC reading rockets up, you know that the CO reading just prior to the HC increase – where you lifted off and pumped the pedal – is the reading that you want.

If you use a Lambda mixture reader, the change in mixture reading is more or less instant, and you needn't resort to any tricks like pumping the pedal, just take a snap-shot reading. When you are happy that the mixture is safe, you can record a power run on the rolling road, right across the rpm range, watching the mixture as you do so.

Once you have established a base line, you can go up and down on main jets, comparing power curves. The 'correct' mixture is the one that gives the best power – simple as that. Don't aim for a specific CO or Lambda reading unless you know for sure that this is what the engine wants to see.

Some of the older iron engines, the Ford Pinto for example, like a lot of fuel, and I find they give the best power on a rich mixture, around 6% CO. Later Ford engines, like the CVH, seem to like much weaker mixtures to make maximum power, sometimes as low as 2.5% CO. The power output is always the final bench mark for correct mixture ratio.

If you have data logging on your Lambda mixture reader, you can check the mixture ratio across the rpm range. As a general rule, you can tip the fuelling at very high rpm by altering the air-corrector jet. I always start with an air-corrector jet two steps up on main-jet size. If the mixture is a little weak at maximum rpm, you can close down the air corrector to compensate. You need quite large changes in air-corrector jet size compared to changing main jets. The ratio is roughly three-to-one. Three steps on the air corrector gives the same mixture change as one main-jet size. It is easier to fine tune with the air corrector than the main jet.

Fig. 9.8. A Dellorto accelerator pump assembly.

Be wary of going too small on the air corrector. If you get too little air entering the emulsion tube, this can result in a very poorly emulsified mixture; 'too wet' as I once heard it described. The result is a misfire that can be hard to track down. Certain Dellorto 'emission' carbs are very sensitive to smaller air-corrector sizes, resulting in a misfire bad enough to stop you taking a power curve.

Emulsion tube selection

The numbering system for Weber emulsion tubes takes no logical form that I can decipher. Dellortos are much more straightforward. It would appear that the Weber factory simply made up numbers in

Fig. 9.9. Emulsion tubes.

the order that tubes were developed for different applications. Basically, the variables are the number of air-bleed holes and their position, and the thickness of the tube.

For Weber carbs, if in doubt, start with F16. This is about the richest tube in the range, and a rich mixture covers a multitude of sins. Slightly weaker in the mid-range is the F11, and slightly richer is the F7. The only real way to find the right, or best, tube for your engine is to run it on the rolling road/dyno and check the results.

For Dellorto carbs, the emulsion tubes are given the part number 7772, and the number relating to the air bleed comes next. For example, 7772.3 is a very rich tube, while 7772.7 is much weaker. Tubes go up in steps of 0.1, the higher the number, the weaker the tube. The way to remember it is; bigger number equals bigger air bleed – and hence weaker mixture.

I run a power curve with a given emulsion tube, and then substitute the tube, but keep the air and main jets the same. Check the lambda mixture reader as the engine runs across the rpm range, and then compare the power curves. The best tube is simply the one that gives the best power across the rpm operating range.

Although not officially recommended, you can experiment by soldering up emulsion tube air bleed holes. Fill in the higher holes to pull more fuel off earlier and fill the lower holes to richen the top end rpm. Solder can be removed by re-drilling, but check the hole sizes *before* you fill them in.

Accelerator-pump jets (accel-pump jets, or acceleration jets)

Most people run accel-pump jets far too large. Since the amount of fuel injected, and the duration of the injection, is so small in the overall scheme of things, this

Fig. 9.10. Auxiliary venturis.

doesn't really do any harm. Theoretically you should fit the smallest pump jets that mask the flat-spot on snap throttle opening. Since the engine accelerates at its fastest under a no-load condition, you can check this by quickly opening the throttle from idle with the car stationary.

Remember that fuel is drawn from the accel-pump jet at high rpm, and many people use this as a way of richening the top end fuelling. Fitting a slightly large accel-pump jet isn't a problem as long as it doesn't cause black-smoking on snap throttle opening.

It is possible to alter the way in which the pump jet operates by changing the bleed-back valve in the bottom of the float chamber. A smaller bleed-back valve will inject the same amount of fuel but over a longer period. It's very unlikely that you will have a problem with accel fuelling, or will need to alter the supplied bleed-back valve.

When changing pump jets, note the little aluminium washer that forms the seal around the jet. Sometimes this can be left stuck inside the carb, rather than coming out with the jet. This isn't a problem, but don't add a second washer thinking that the first is lost.

Auxiliary venturis (aux vents)

The auxiliary venturi plays an important role in how the main fuelling system works. Air speed through the aux vent is what creates the vacuum signal to draw off fuel. However, there is a limited range of diameters available for each carb size, so your options are fairly limited. The aux vent should only be experimented with if conventional jetting does not produce the desired results.

A smaller aux vent will bring the main system in earlier, a larger one later. Longer and shorter aux vents were introduced to overcome a particular problem with one original equipment application. A pulse was being reflected unfavourably by the standard-length tube, so longer ones were produced to move the reflected length out of the operating range of the engine. It is extremely unlikely that you will encounter this problem.

Pulse tuning

This is a very straightforward 'suck-it-and-see' exercise. Take a power curve, and then change the inlet trumpet length. Note that it is the length that makes the difference here, rather than the shape. Theoretically, a shallow taper gives the best airflow, but airflow isn't the whole story. To get the maximum pulse effect from the induction system, you need the most rapid change in section possible. This is a straight tube opening into atmosphere. Straight bell-mouths with a small radius on the entry give the strongest pulse, and therefore the biggest power gain, at their effective rpm point. The shallow-taper type tends to spread the effect wider across the effective rev range. Every engine is different, so you have to experiment. Take a full power curve to see the effect right across the rpm operating range. You never get gains without losses – somewhere. If the losses are at a

point where you don't run the engine, then you don't have a problem. I would suggest changes in length in steps of 0.5 inches (13.7mm) if you really want to zero-in on the optimum length.

Please don't kid yourself that this pulse tuning isn't important. With one of my 2.0 litre Pinto engines producing 210bhp, I could increase power at 5000rpm by 20% with a two-inch change in overall tract length – two inches longer than the length that gave peak power at 7600rpm. Maximum power dropped by 10bhp, but on a twisty circuit this was a good trade-off to make. With a CVH engine we could change the dips for troughs just by changing the trumpet length, as shown in the power graph below.

If you decide to experiment, you will have to fix your intake

trumpets securely in place – simply retaining them with tape doesn't work. Initially, you might think that the air passing into the engine will hold them in place, but it won't. The trumpets try to move away from the engine because of the partial vacuum that surrounds their intake area – effectively they get sucked out of the carb. If you want the best from your carbs, then pulse tuning the intake lengths isn't something that you can afford to ignore.

Be aware that at some stage you will run into a 'bad length', whereby a lot of fuel mist appears around the inlet trumpet. If this happens outside your engine's operating power band it isn't a problem, although bear in mind that it might cause a fire hazard if the fuel is trapped inside the air filter.

Fig. 9.11. These graphs show the effect of different intake lengths on a CVH engine.

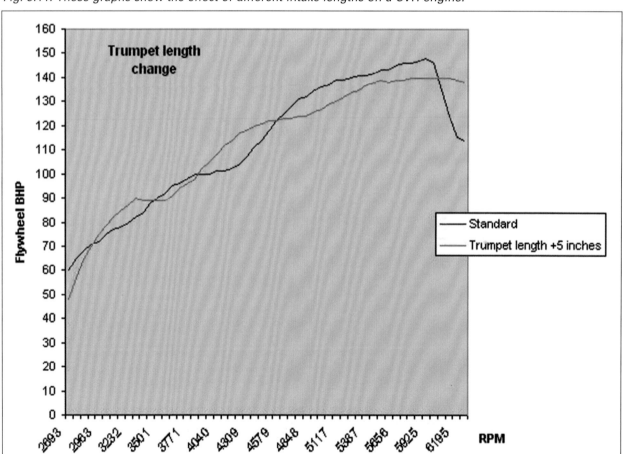

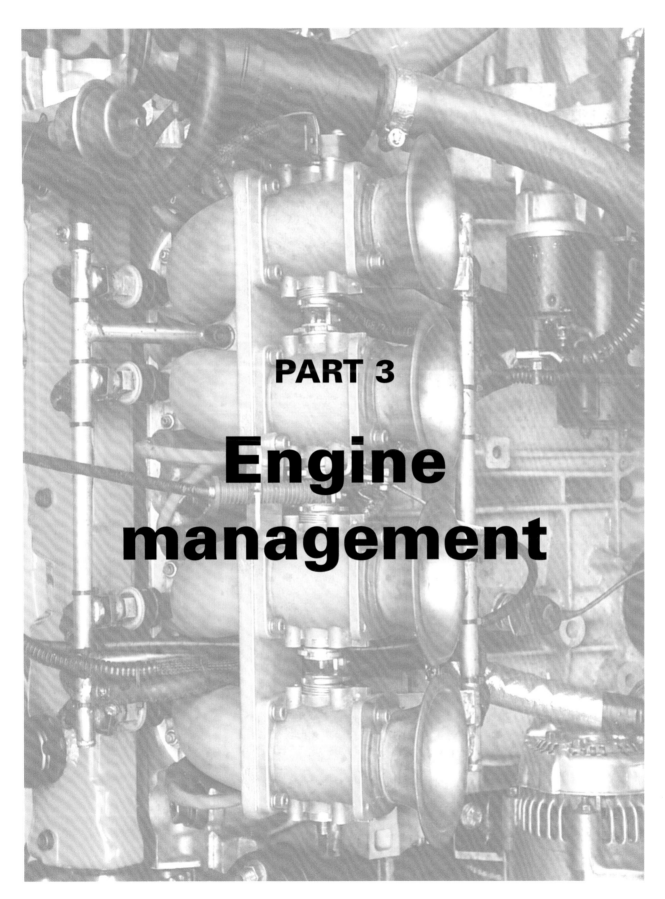

PART 3

Engine management

Chapter 10
Engine management theory

Introduction

Afraid? A lot of people are. Mention engine management and they go running off to hide behind their carburettors and clockwork ignition, complaining about cost and complexity. The reality is that engine management is much simpler to work with than carburettors and advance weights – once you know how. This is how it works.

In the beginning...

Original equipment (OE) mechanical injection systems

The very first injection systems used a mechanical pump, not unlike an in-line diesel pump, to inject fuel directly into the combustion chamber. In the 1950s when Jaguar and Mercedes were slugging it out on the tracks, mechanical injection was a must-have for any self-respecting works racing team. Initially it was reserved for state-of-the-art cars, but in the 1970s Lucas came up with their mechanical injection system for mass production, and this was used by the Triumph Motor Company (a division of British Leyland). The system used a high-pressure electric pump in the fuel line, and a rotating delivery head – similar to a rotary diesel injection pump. A cam operated a pair of pistons that compressed the

Fig. 10.1. ECUs that you can re-map from the computer have opened up the world of fuel injection to the amateur engine builder.

Fig. 10.2. Lucas mechanical injection – not the most reliable start to the injection era.

Fig. 10.3. The Bosch Jetronic metering head supplied fuel as a constant spray, rather than as a timed injection phase.

fuel just as the outlet ports lined up in the pump. The piston stroke then varied the amount of fuel delivered. This was a sequential system of some sophistication compared to the alternative SU or Stromberg carburettors.

However, it was to prove too complicated for the average dealer, and a lot of the systems were junked in favour of SU carburettors, which although not perfect in themselves, did give a lot less trouble.

Injection remained pretty much a diesel thing for years, until it exploded onto the scene in the early '80s. Bosch came up with the 'Jetronic' injection system, which wasn't really an injection system at all. It was more akin to a fuel-spraying device, which pumped fuel in a continuous stream into the inlet manifold, albeit close to the inlet valve. The biggest advantage was that it overcame fuel distribution problems and also fuel dropout, since the manifold was essentially left dry.

Fuel metering was via a vast moving flap in the inlet system. This flap was connected to a metering head by a mechanical arm. The head contained a fuel delivery valve with slits, which were exposed as the air flap lifted the metering lever. The marketing people got hold of the idea and added an 'i' to the end of the model number. If you didn't have a GTi or an XRi in the 1980s you were a very sad individual indeed.

For engine modifiers it was a nightmare. Any sort of modified cam gave the moving flap fits, and conventional airflow enhancing tricks soon found the fuel delivery limitations of the system. It was some years before people started to get into raising base fuel-line pressures or altering the metering head to try to tailor the fuel slope to a new requirement. Twin '40s still ruled! Then Bosch added some electronics to the system, and people started to talk about the death of the tuning industry!

Electronic systems

Electronic OE injection systems do not generally use throttle butterfly angle for reading load. Most systems use some form of airflow measurement. In theory this is the best way to decide how much fuel to add to the engine. If you have X amount of air, it will always need Y amount of fuel to give the required mixture ratio. Theoretically the system doesn't need to know what the engine is doing or even what the rpm of the engine is, it simply looks at the airflow and adds the appropriate amount of fuel.

The first electronic-injection engines using airflow meters still had an engine link to read rpm, plus coolant and air temperature. The ignition side of things was taken care of by a conventional distributor and ignition system. The airflow meter supplied the main fuelling base, but they still had to run an injection map stored in the ECU. Measuring airflow is nice, but the engine doesn't always play the game. Often it takes in air, and passes some of it out of the exhaust. Sometimes the air travels through the meter, but reverses back out, rather than getting as far as the engine. We refer to this phenomenon as the 'volumetric efficiency' (VE) of the engine. VE maps allow the system to compensate for these airflow management problems.

The device for measuring airflow started out as a simple moving flap. Working against a spring, the air pulled into the engine moved the flap and a variable resistor told the ECU how far it had moved. As the airflow dropped away, the spring returned the flap to its starting point. The flap needed a small balance chamber to reduce fluctuations or pulses in the induction system, but it worked quite well.

From an engine modifier's viewpoint it wasn't too wonderful. The flap proved to be restrictive to increased airflow above the design maximum, but at least you had a relatively easy way of adjusting the overall fuelling. The spring tension on the flap was adjustable via a ratchet mechanism so, once you had prised the top off the unit, you could adjust the mixture in given steps to alter the fuelling. This was

Fig. 10.4. The L-Jetronic airflow meter retained a moving flap design, connected directly to the fuel metering head.

Fig. 10.5. The K-Jetronic flap was connected to a sliding resistance which told the ECU how far the flap had moved.

an overall adjustment, but it was cheaper than going to a chip company!

Later airflow meters are known as 'hot wire' meters. These meters work by passing a known current through a wire to bring it to a known temperature. Any air passing over the wire cools it, and more current is needed to return the wire temperature to its base setting. Thus airflow is directly related to the current flowing through the wire.

The metering wire is set to one side of the main airflow, with just a proportion of the air diverted to pass over the wire, or the wire might be set into a venturi in the centre of the main airflow. Either way, the total flow was less restricted, and designers could afford to be more generous with the flow capability, and still maintain accurate monitoring.

Now we have the 'bubble', or film sensor. Basically, a bubble of air is trapped between two thin films of material. As the air pressure in which the bubble sits varies, the bubble expands and contracts. Link the bubble to the inlet manifold, and this expansion and contraction then relates directly to manifold inlet pressure – and manifold inlet

Fig. 10.6. Hot wire airflow meter. Airflow cools the wire which needs more current to maintain temperature. Hence the current flow is related to airflow.

Fig. 10.7. MAP sensor. Manifold air pressure directly relates to airflow and this sensor offers no resistance to the engine's breathing.

pressure relates directly to airflow. The bubble's changing dimensions are measured electronically, and this information is passed to the ECU, where the VE maps are used to take care of the fuelling corrections.

Finally, we have Manifold Air Pressure (MAP) sensor-based airflow measurement. The MAP sensor is an electronic device which performs the same job as the film sensor, or 'bubble'. It measures air pressure in the manifold (some would say lack of air pressure), and relates this to air pressure outside the manifold. If you have a pressure-charged engine, you need a sensor that measures positive pressure as well

as vacuum. The degree of positive pressure measurement available will dictate the maximum boost that you can obtain and still be measuring airflow.

Fuelling theory

Basics

With a carburettor you rely on engine vacuum to pull fuel from a well. With fuel injection you supply fuel from a pressurised source and squirt it into the engine – as simple as that. But getting the right amount of fuel into the engine under all operating conditions requires a bit more sophistication. Electronic fuel injection has only been possible with the

Fig. 10.8a. Screen maps show the fuel . . .

M3D - Elise14.fig

File Connection Additional settings Graph Setup Help

Speed Sites

		0	500	1,000	1,500	2,000	2,500	3,000	3,500	4,000	4,500
	0	55	39	28	27	26	25	22	20	20	17
	1	70	65	61	53	46	41	42	39	37	33
	2	88	80	75	70	58	54	51	50	50	47
	3	93	85	80	80	67	65	62	61	60	58
	4	98	90	85	85	75	73	75	71	67	65
	5	98	90	85	85	77	78	78	79	81	75
	6	98	90	85	87	79	83	86	88	90	85
	7	100	92	87	89	79	84	90	93	96	90
	8	100	92	87	87	78	82	92	92	100	99
	9	100	92	87	85	78	82	92	92	100	101
	10	100	92	87	85	78	82	92	92	101	101
	11	100	92	87	85	79	82	92	95	101	101
	12	100	92	87	85	79	82	92	95	102	102

Load Sites

Injection map

\Details \Events \Ignition \Injection \Idle control \Air temp \Coolant temp \Live adjustments \

| 17:21 | Speed site : 2 (1000 - 1500 rpm) | Status - ECU connected |

development of the solenoid-operated fuel injector. The electronic injector unit is nothing more than a solenoid valve. Fuel under pressure is supplied to the valve, and fuel flow takes place when the valve (injector) is opened. Opening the injector for a given time at a given pressure results in a measured amount of fuel being squirted into the inlet manifold.

The injector opens and closes (pulses) very rapidly in time with engine rpm. The pulse is always linked to engine speed, but the amount of fuel injected is varied by making the pulse duration (the time for which the injector is open) longer or shorter. This 'pulse width

modulation' principle is the key to electronic injection.

Now we have to decide how much fuel is introduced into the engine and exactly when. This is where the Electronic Control Unit (ECU) comes into play. Stored in the ECU is a reference grid. Engine speed will be along one side of the grid, engine load along the other. The computer looks at engine speed and load information supplied by sensors, and selects the figure in the relevant box of the grid. These grids of numbers are sometimes called 'look-up tables', but most people simply call them 'maps'. The number of grid boxes or 'sites' in a map can vary depending on the system. For

speed sites it is common to have one site every 500rpm, although some systems can have more. The load, or throttle opening, is divided into steps from idle to full throttle. Competition systems can have anything from eight load sites to 12 or 16 sites. The more sites you have, the longer it takes to fill them all in with the right numbers.

The actual number of sites does not relate to the number of references that the computer uses. The map sites are only the points within the overall map that you can alter. The computer looks at many points in between the map sites. This is called 'interpolation'. If you put the number 20 in one site, and 30 in the next, the computer does

Fig. 10.8b . . . and ignition settings that the engine will 'look up' during normal running.

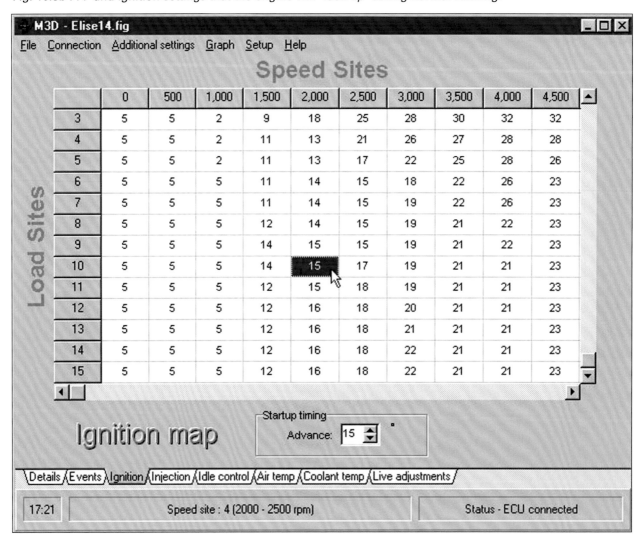

not jump from one to the other. It looks at the points between and moves in steps from 20 towards 30 in a smooth progression. Effectively, it draws a line between the two points, both in the direction of speed sites and load sites.

When trying to adjust a map site, it pays to bear in mind that you have to have the engine exactly on the site you want to adjust, otherwise you are only moving the line between points, tipping it in one direction or the other.

The sensors that tell the ECU how fast the engine is running, and how much throttle is applied, can vary enormously in their mode of operation. The engine speed signal can come from a distributor or a toothed wheel mounted on the camshaft or crankshaft. In the case of the toothed wheel, basically a small magnetic pick-up generates a pulse, which the ECU can count. If the system knows how many teeth on the wheel correspond to one revolution of the crankshaft, then it can count engine rpm. Having multiple teeth means that the ECU does not have to wait for one whole revolution before it can calculate engine rpm, the system is constantly updating.

Engine load is indicated simply by how much air is entering the engine past the throttle. This can be measured with many different types of airflow sensors. These can be moving flaps (early road systems) hot-wire sensors, MAP sensors, or combinations of the above. For competition use, the majority of systems use a sensor that simply reads throttle angle. As the throttle is opened by a given amount, the sensor angle reading is linked to a site in the engine map. Each time the throttle reaches this particular angle, the same map reference is fed into the system.

Throttle angle does not relate directly to airflow, but it is very close. In the early days of throttle-angle-based competition systems, non-believers pointed at the car

manufacturer's products and smugly stated that none of them used throttle angle. The cry was 'inaccurate'. Now one major manufacturer has fitted a throttle-angle system to its production-line product. The fact is, measuring throttle angle works better from a driver's perspective, in terms of throttle response, than any other system.

Since the amount of fuel injected depends on the amount of air ingested, it stands to reason that anything which alters the volume of air entering the engine must be compensated for by altering the fuelling to suit. The biggest cause of a change in air volume, apart from opening the throttle, is going to be air temperature. As we saw earlier, hot air is less dense than cold air. If the air temperature under the bonnet, or at the intake, increases, then less air effectively enters the engine. With computer control we can measure the temperature of the air entering the engine, and put a correction into the fuel map to keep the mixture constant. Theoretically, this is a fixed correction to allow for air expansion, and therefore some ECUs have an automatic correction factor built in. Others give you a choice of correction so that you can fine-tune the system for different engine designs. In practice this is rarely necessary.

The biggest correction has to be

for coolant temperature. With a cold engine you obviously need more fuel (this is provided by the choke on a carburettor), and this enrichment must reduce as the engine warms up. With most, but not all, engine-management systems, you can fine-tune the warm up mixture slope. The amount of fuel correction required will vary depending on the injectors used, the base fuel-line pressure, and the design of the inlet manifold. It isn't possible to have a fixed correction factor for all engines as you can with air correction.

The last correction can be for air pressure. At sea level air is denser than at altitude, and you can use a pressure sensor to measure air pressure and correct the fuel and ignition to suit. This is one of those 'fixed' corrections that you don't need to map. If you put your sensor in the intake air box, then any pressure build up due to 'ram effect' (forward motion of the car) will also be compensated for. Personally, I've never had a car that moves fast enough to gain any positive air box pressure – I've been told you need in excess of 160mph!

Injection theory

The injectors can be triggered in different ways. All the injectors can be triggered once every engine revolution (batch fired), individual

Fig. 10.9. Injectors share a common fuel rail in most installations.

injectors can be triggered on inlet valve opening (sequential), or they can be triggered in pairs (semi-sequential). Each method of triggering has both advantages and disadvantages when used on a competition engine.

Starting with batch firing of the injectors, with this method the fuel is introduced into the inlet manifold in two stages relative to the engine's four-stroke cycle (the four-stroke cycle takes two revolutions of the engine). All the injectors trigger once every engine revolution. Half the fuel is injected during each revolution and, depending on the cylinder's firing order, fuel may be injected with the inlet valve open or closed. During the next revolution, again half the fuel is injected, but the valves are in different positions. From a power output perspective it makes almost no difference which valves are open or closed when the fuel starts to inject.

Sequential injection is when the fuel is injected according to the inlet valve position. Each injector fires in turn, and the injector firing can be timed to the point of inlet valve opening, or any other point that might be required. With this system, all the fuel for a particular cylinder has to be injected in one single shot.

Semi-sequential injection (on a four-cylinder engine) is when the four injectors are fired in two pairs. The injectors are linked 1/4 and 2/3, which is closer to sequential than batch-firing, but it's still only semi-sequential. The Rover K-Series engine uses a semi-sequential set-up as standard with the original-equipment MEMS engine management system.

For a competition engine, the biggest advantage of sequential injection is the reduced fuel consumption. With big overlap camshafts, when the engine is operating 'off cam', a lot of the air drawn into the cylinder is lost straight out of the exhaust. With batch fired systems, that lost air also includes some of the injected fuel. With a sequential system, if you have the facility to alter the triggering point you can time the fuel delivery to ensure that all the fuel remains in the cylinder. Trigger too soon, and you lose most of the fuel, trigger too late and you don't fill the cylinder but leave the fuel trapped against a closed inlet valve. However, this only applies, in the main, to part throttle operating conditions.

With competition engines running close to maximum injector duration at high rpm, the time available for injection is limited. This means that there isn't the time available to get all the fuel injected during the inlet valve open period. As a result, the sequential system has no advantage over batch firing under these conditions.

The next consideration is fuel presentation. In theory you want to break down the fuel into tiny droplets that will mix with the air and burn cleanly. From an emissions viewpoint you want to vaporise the fuel. This can be done by aiming the injector to squirt on to the back of the closed (hot) inlet valve. With batch firing you have the opportunity for the fuel to pick up heat from the induction tract while it is waiting to be drawn into the engine.

From a power perspective this is the last thing you want. You certainly need to break the fuel down, but any vaporising action is there for a different reason. If the fuel is allowed to take heat from the surrounding air, that air is cooled. A cooler air charge means a denser charge – quite simply you get more air into the cylinder per induction stroke, and this results in more power.

In order to achieve this you have to give the fuel the maximum possible chance of mixing with the air. This is achieved in two ways. First you need time for this to happen, secondly you need fuel dispersal within the air charge. You can achieve both these objectives by placing the injector as far away from the inlet valve as possible. As the fuel enters the air stream it has more time available for drawing heat from the air, because it has further to travel to reach the inlet valve. Also, because it has more distance to travel, it has a better chance of mixing within the air charge. This practice is known as 'upstream injection'.

The down side to upstream injection is that at low air speeds this extra time and distance involved in the fuel reaching the inlet valve works against you. At low rpm and small throttle opening the fuel drops out of the slow moving air, and puddles on the floor of the induction system.

What you are looking for in order to extract maximum power is something engineers call 'shear effect'. You want the incoming air to break up, or shear, the fuel droplets. Theoretically the shear effect can be improved by pointing the injector away from the engine, firing the fuel against the incoming air stream. To some extent this does work, but there are other problems with reverse injection. At low engine rpm the fuel overcomes the incoming air speed, and a lot escapes, collecting outside the engine. Fuel builds up in the filter or air-box, and the first time you have a spit-back up the intake, this fuel quickly catches fire. Although it is theoretically correct to reverse the injector direction, it seldom proves practical to do so.

The most practical solution is to have two injectors per cylinder, one fitted close to the engine, and aimed at the inlet valve, the other as far away from the engine as possible. At low air speed/engine rpm only the inner injector triggers. At wide-open throttle you run both inner and outer injectors – you do not switch from one to the other. Practical tests have proved that by running both injectors you get the benefit of cooling the air charge, plus by injecting fuel at two points in the air stream you get better mixing of the fuel charge throughout the air.

Fig. 10.10. The injection direction plays its part in power production. Here the injector is angled at approximately 45° to the airflow.

Dyno tests carried out on my own rolling road showed that you can't switch on the outer injectors at too low an air speed. With my own development system, we switched on the injectors only at higher rpm – *and only at wide open throttle*. High rpm with small throttle opening still results in low air speed, you need engine speed and load for the outer injectors to be effective. If you don't take this precaution, you will find that fuel coming from the outer injector simply drops out of the air stream and you get a big weak-mixture flat-spot.

In order to prevent any 'flutter' at the injector change-over point

Fig. 10.11. Double injectors are the best compromise on injector position, giving just about the best of both worlds.

(as the second injector cuts in and out), the software should include some hysteresis. Switch-on of the second injector should always be at least 50rpm above the switch-off point. The software can take care of this automatically, all you need is the facility to select the switch-on rpm point. I found that by halving the injector duration as the second injector comes in, you can simply experiment to find the best rpm change point. You can then forget about the switching and just map in the normal way.

The end result of running double injectors in this manner is an undetectable switch-over from singles to doubles, and a gain in peak bhp; typically over 4%.

Injector sequencing

You hear a lot of talk about sequential and semi-sequential injection or batch firing. These terms refer to the number of times the injectors are triggered during the four-stroke cycle. The theory is that since a carburettor only takes in fuel during the induction stroke, carried in on the incoming air stream, then the injection cycle should match this flow of fuel.

Early Bosch mechanical injection systems had a continuous spray from the injector (K-Jetronic) while the first Lucas mechanical injection was actually timed. I once saw figures from a Lucas system with the triggering 180° out, and it made no discernible difference to the power output.

Batch-triggered injectors are fired twice per cycle, ie every 360° of the crankshaft, and all the injectors fire together. The triggering event has nothing to do with the inlet valve opening or closing point. Any fuel that isn't drawn into the engine on the first induction stroke hangs around in the inlet port waiting for the next. This might not sound very clever, but it works extremely well for a number of reasons. First you do not need injectors with very big flow capacity, because you are effectively putting the fuel into the engine in two halves. This gives you finer control over the fuel, as each step in the software amounts to a smaller amount of fuel being injected, a finer resolution in fact. Next, the fuel hanging around in the inlet has a chance to pick up some heat from the manifold walls. This helps to vaporise the fuel, and you get less 'wet' mixture entering the engine.

The down side is that you can be wasting fuel when the engine is running inefficiently, blowing fuel out of the exhaust when not all the inducted air is trapped in the cylinder. Think of it this way: if your engine inducts 1lb of air, but only half of it gets trapped in the combustion chamber (there will be some blow-through into the exhaust) you still need to add enough fuel for 1lb of air, hence half of the fuel is wasted. Exhaust hydrocarbon emissions are also very high in this instance.

The semi-sequential system triggers the injectors in pairs on a four-cylinder engine. Instead of firing all four injectors every 360°, you can link injectors 1 and 3, and then 2 and 4 together, or 1 and 2, and 3 and 4 (which is more convenient). This method triggers two injectors every 720°. The easy way to get your head around it is to think of the four cycles, or strokes. Cylinders 1 and 2 go suck/suck, nothing/nothing, while 3 and 4 go nothing/nothing, suck/suck.

On a fully sequential system you get a firing event every 180°, but only one injector is triggered at a time. This allows you to have individual fuelling for every cylinder. Obviously you then have to get all the fuel into the engine during the induction stroke – which limits the time available. Sequential systems generally need larger flowing injectors than batch-fired systems. The timing of the injector can be varied, so that you do not end up fuelling the air that blows through to the exhaust. In this way you get better fuel consumption and less hydrocarbon emissions. Logically the injector

event needs to be finished by the time the inlet valve closes, so the injection timing needs to be adjustable on a competition management system – if you change the camshaft, you need to change the fuel event timing.

For a competition engine the batch-firing system works. There are theoretical advantages over sequential injection in some areas, and advantages for sequential in others. On the cars that I have mapped to date, there's very little to choose between batch-fired and sequential injection in terms of power output and driveability.

Direct injection

The current trend in engine design is towards direct injection. This has nothing to do with power; it's a fuel economy move and little else. However, it seems prudent to cover the basic theory here, since these engines will start to get modified at some stage.

In order to inject petrol directly into the combustion chamber the injection system has to run at very high pressure. The chamber and piston are designed so that at TDC they form a little pocket directly underneath the spark plug. By timing the injection to introduce the fuel as this pocket forms, most of the fuel stays in this confined area, rather than spreading around the combustion chamber. This results in a rich mixture being formed in the area of the spark plug. This starts combustion, which then spreads across the chamber to the very weak mixtures on the extremes of the chamber. Since it is very hard to initiate combustion with a weak mixture, this 'stratified charge' system is the only way to run very weak mixtures without misfires.

This is a very important point, because misfires send raw fuel down the exhaust to the catalytic converter (cat), where it burns and increases the internal temperature of the cat. This in turn can lead to fires starting up underneath the car, as well as ruining the cat!

When full power is required, the stratified charge is a liability, because to get the overall mixture right within the chamber, you would end up with a super-rich mixture under the plug, again leading to misfires. The answer is to inject the fuel earlier, so that it spreads about the chamber long before the piston reaches TDC and forms its pocket under the spark plug.

You can see from this that the timing of the injection is critical, and that sequential injection is a must, since each cylinder has to be timed in sequence. You can also see that the time available for injection at high rpm is very limited. You can't start injection until the exhaust stroke is over, and it has to end well before the top of the compression stroke if the stratified charge effect is to be avoided. This means that the incoming fuel has to work against cylinder pressure, as well as arrive in a very short (relative) time period. This explains the very high fuel line pressures involved in a direct injection engine, and why only a sequential system will do.

BL 'A-Series' engine – a special case

Engines work by pumping air, and in order to pump larger volumes of air you need larger ports. Before someone figured out that you can have larger ports if you put inlet and exhaust ports on opposite sides of the cylinder head, the answer was to have fewer ports. The British came up with the five-port head in the A-Series engine by using a shared (siamesed) inlet port for two cylinders.

Since each of the two cylinders takes its turn to use the inlet port, this isn't as restrictive as you might imagine – hence power outputs of over 100bhp/litre on race versions of this engine. This arrangement is fine with carburettors, but when you use fuel injection you run into problems with the shared inlet ports. With conventional batch-

Fig. 10.12. The trusty A-Series engine can be kitted out with electronic injection to great effect – even turbo conversions.

fired injection, fuel is injected once every engine revolution. As previously described, half the required fuel goes in each time the injector pulses, and the fuel hangs around in the inlet port until the valve opens. With the A-Series you have two inlet ports, and hence only two injectors.

The big problem is that while the fuel is 'hanging around', waiting for number one inlet valve to open, the inlet valve on number two cylinder opens and robs the charge. When the second half of the fuel arrives, this goes into the open inlet on number two cylinder, and number one cylinder never sees any fuel. You end up with an engine running on two cylinders. What actually happens is that some fuel finds its way into the robbed cylinders, but only enough to idle the engine. The engine fires on all four cylinders, but develops no power as you increase the revs – ask me how I know!

To make life interesting the problem actually moves around,

sometimes cylinders one and four run okay, sometimes two and three. This is a random problem depending on which cylinders line up with the phasing of the injectors on start up.

The answer is to double the pulse phasing and then halve the pulse width. You inject fuel every 180° instead of every 360°, but only half as much in each pulse. Two of the four pulses go to each cylinder, and you get even distribution – or at least as even as the original carburettor was.

Rover went a different route. They started with a single injector system, and then went to dual injectors, but with some tricky software to overcome the distribution problem of the five-port head. In order to reproduce a sequential type of system, each pulse is timed to the inlet valve, and the fuel is injected in one long pulse. The problem here is that when the pulse duration gets longer, the pulses overlap. One pulse hasn't finished putting fuel in

when the next pulse is required to start. Rover came up with some software which kept the time between the two pulses constant. When the pulse duration needs to be longer, the first pulse is simply started sooner, while the second pulse still starts the same time after the first pulse, but is extended for longer. That way the finish/start time remains constant and the two pulses do not overlap.

This system allowed Rover to continue using the A-Series engine for a few more years and still meet emissions regulations. You have to assume that with the original design first appearing in the 1940s Rover felt that they hadn't had their money's worth out of it yet!

Pulse tuning theory

When air moves through a pipe it can produce a sound wave. This is how many musical instruments work, the trumpet for example. When an engine runs, it draws air through the throttle body, and in doing so creates a sound wave. This sound wave has energy which can be used to increase engine performance. The wave starts at the engine intake valve and moves towards the intake trumpet. On reaching the end of the trumpet (more commonly called a bell-mouth) this wave is reflected, changing sign and direction. The result is a positive pulse moving towards the engine. This pulse will carry air and fuel into the engine. It works like free supercharging, forcing air and fuel into the engine.

The overall length of the intake system from valve to bell-mouth entry determines the engine rpm at which this positive pulse effect takes place. Unfortunately, there will also be an engine rpm where the effect is negative, with fuel and air being pushed *out* of the engine. This can often be seen on wide-open throttle as a fuel mist, blowing around inside the intake trumpets.

We need to find the best compromise on tract length that makes optimum use of the positive pulse, while putting the negative pulse at an rpm where the engine does not normally run. With most throttle-body systems we can tune the pulse length simply by changing the length of the intake trumpet. Some engine builders have a 'favourite' bell-mouth which they use on everything, but you must remember that it is the *overall length* which determines the pulse effect. Use a shorter, or longer, inlet manifold and the overall length changes, altering the tuned length of the system.

In order to maximise the pulse-tuning effect, you need to keep changes in section to a minimum. Stepping up from a small-bore inlet manifold to a large-bore throttle body, for example, should be avoided. This is another good reason for not selecting too large a throttle body.

Finally, some engine 'experts' will tell you that longer trumpets give better mid-range power, and shorter ones give maximum top-

Fig. 10.13. Changing the intake lengths can have a big effect on the final shape of the power curve. The intake length includes the lengths of the intake trumpet, throttle body, manifold and intake porting.

Fig. 10.14. With most throttle-body systems we can tune the pulse length simply by changing the length of the intake trumpet.

end power – don't listen to them. This can be the case, but equally if your intake system is over-long, or over-short, you can gain power in unexpected places by going shorter or longer. On sensitive engines you often find that a power curve is like a wave as it climbs the graph. Changing the length of the trumpets will move the dips and bumps to a different rpm, so what you gain on the swings you lose on the roundabouts. Sometimes that's life.

Closed-loop systems and lambda sensors

When exhaust emissions started to become a major political issue, car manufacturers were forced to look at ways of reducing the exhaust carbon monoxide (CO) output. The answer was a catalytic converter. The big problem with the catalyst is that it needs an exact, and chemically correct, mixture burning in the engine before it can deal with the resulting exhaust gas. This requirement is almost impossible to achieve with carburettors – calibration really isn't that accurate with a carburettor.

However, with electronic injection the mixture can be controlled under all operating conditions, and to control the mixture in order to use a catalyst,

what is needed is some form of feed-back to the management system so that it knows what is happening to the mixture after it has burnt. Thus the lambda sensor was born. This sensor has a probe that extends into the exhaust gas stream and generates a voltage signal which is dependent on the amount of oxygen present in the exhaust gas. This signal can be directly related to mixture ratio. Early lambda sensors had just two wires to carry the signal voltage.

The signal voltage range is very small, from 0.2 volts to 0.8 volts, and early sensors were really only accurate in the middle of this range. As the sensor technology improved, the manufacturers tried harder and harder to 'zero in' on the operating range to make the critical chemically correct (stoichiometric) area more accurate – to the obvious detriment of the wider operating range of the sensor.

The sensor needs heat in order to generate the voltage, and an engine on cold start takes a while to bring the sensor up to temperature. To get the sensor working sooner, the first trick manufacturers used was to run the ignition very retarded when the engine was cold (the ECU receives a signal from a coolant temperature sensor). Then they tried to locate the sensor closer to the exhaust port. But the best trick

was to add an electric heating element to the sensor. This gave us three wires on the sensor, and by adding a shielding wire to reduce electronic interference you end up with a four-wire sensor.

The signal from this sensor is passed to the engine's ECU so that the relevant stoichiometric mixture ratio can be maintained. In reality, the mixture isn't held at one precise ratio, rather it swings from rich to lean across the sensor operating range to give an average mixture which is correct for the catalyst. This operating system is called 'closed loop' because it is a continuous cycle of correction and feed-back.

The emissions are not controlled by the closed-loop system all the time. Because we need different mixture ratios for cold starting, acceleration and full power, the closed-loop system only really operates at idle and under light cruise conditions. This point has not been made to the wider public, because it might call into question the effectiveness of the catalytic converter – not what politicians and motor manufacturers want at all!

As manufacturers look for more and more fuel-efficient engines, mixture ratios need to be weaker to suit the direct-injection engine (which is designed to run weaker mixtures). This has resulted in the development of lambda sensors that have a wider operating range which, finally, is the good news for us.

The wide-range lambda sensors enable us to link the sensor to a meter, which shows us the mixture ratio. This can be shown on a computer screen, on a row of light-emitting diodes, or on an analogue meter. Either way, it allows us to map an engine using the lambda sensor to tell us exactly what the mixture is doing. At the time of writing, these wide-range sensors are very expensive, and the slope-corrected hardware needed to give you an accurate reading is also out of the price range of the

Fig. 10.15. The lambda sensor reads the oxygen content of the exhaust gas and relates this to mixture strength.

average enthusiast. However, some companies are already working on mixture readers to utilize the wide-range lambda sensors from later lean-burn technology engines. When they become widely available, these tools will be invaluable to the tuner when mapping an engine.

Ignition timing theory

Basic principles

Ignition control via an ECU is probably *more* beneficial to the engine than fuelling. To understand why, you have to know how the fuel and air burn inside the combustion chamber, and why we require different spark advances for different engine speed and load conditions.

With combustion, it's a little bit like setting fire to a piece of paper. The flame starts at the point of ignition and spreads across the paper from there, until all the paper is consumed.

Let's begin by looking at how combustion inside the engine is supposed to work. Our fuel and air mixture is sitting in the combustion chamber, packed around our sparking plug. A spark arrives at the plug, and the mixture starts to burn at that point. The flame spreads across the mixture until the whole chamber is alight. Obviously this takes time, and at high rpm, time is the one thing we really don't have to spare. The problem we have is that when the engine is running the piston doesn't hang around at TDC for very long. The faster the engine revs, the less time the piston spends at TDC. If the combustion is too slow, the piston is gone before the burning mixture can expand and do any useful work on the piston.

What we have to do to overcome this problem is get the mixture burning faster. One way to speed up burn rate is to compress the mixture before we introduce the spark. All engines have a natural compression ratio of some sort. We

measure the compression ratio by taking the swept volume of the cylinder, adding the combustion chamber volume, and then dividing the answer by the combustion chamber volume. For example: a cylinder has a swept volume of 100cc. The combustion chamber has a volume of 10cc. 100+10 = 110. Divide that by 10 and you get a compression ratio (CR) of 11-to-1.

The higher the compression ratio, the faster the burn – but there are limits. Go too high, and the mixture will suddenly detonate. Detonation is when the mixture 'explodes' rather than burns in a controlled manner. The detonation point will depend on the mixture ratio, the combustion chamber temperature, mixture presentation, and how hot the spark plug is – or a multitude of combinations of the

above. The limit is different for every engine design.

This ideal compression ratio that we are talking about is not a simple calculation. What the engine sees is the *volume* of mixture in the cylinder being squeezed. Put more mixture in, and the compression is effectively higher. We have to set the maximum compression ratio based on the maximum cylinder filling that we can achieve. For example, on light throttle loads the cylinder filling is a lot less, which means the engine would stand a higher compression ratio with that amount of load. But open the throttle, and the cylinder filling increases, requiring a lower mechanical compression ratio. It's a dynamic thing, the goal posts are always moving – so what can we do to get around it?

Fig. 10.16. The compression ratio (CR) can only be measured after measuring the combustion chamber volume with a burette or a graduated cc cylinder.

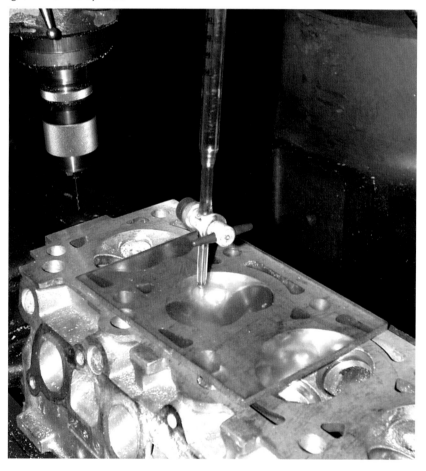

The answer, or more accurately the best answer we can practically come up with, is to alter the point at which we start the combustion process. This is 'ignition timing'.

Since it takes a period of time to get the whole chamber alight, we start the combustion process some time before TDC. The slower the burn rate of the fuel and air mixture, the earlier we start combustion. Ignition timing is therefore quoted in crankshaft degrees before TDC. On very light throttle load (poor cylinder filling), we need more ignition advance than with full throttle load (best possible cylinder filling). That much is pretty obvious, but it gets more complicated. The faster we rev the engine, the less time the piston stays around TDC. Therefore we need to advance the timing more at higher revs. Now we have a three-dimensional timing requirement. The optimum timing will depend not only on how high we rev the engine, but also on how much throttle we have at any particular point in the rev range.

But now we have to consider yet another dimension to the equation. Up to this point we have considered the fuel and air mixture as a static charge, just hanging around waiting for the spark to start the combustion process. In reality the mixture is moving, or swirling about, inside the combustion chamber. This movement of the mixture will cause the flame-front to be carried around the chamber. The intensity of the movement, and especially the direction it takes, will cause the whole mixture to light-up faster than a static charge. Again, the intensity and direction of flame-front movement will depend on how fast the engine is turning and how well we have filled the cylinder. Combustion, as you can see, is a very complex process.

To get the mixture moving inside the chamber, we use the velocity of the incoming charge and also the movement of the piston coming up the bore. When

Fig. 10.17. A close squish area (the area between the piston and cylinder head) speeds up combustion and generates more power – see text for detailed description.

the piston comes close to the cylinder head at TDC, any mixture between the head and the piston gets 'squished' out of the way. We call this area between the piston and cylinder head a 'squish band'. The incoming velocity of the charge, coming from the inlet, creates turbulence which we tend to call 'swirl' or 'tumble'. It is a combination of squish and swirl/tumble that determines how the mixture in the combustion chamber burns.

When a manufacturer develops an engine, experiments are carried out with compression ratio, swirl and squish, to get the best compromise for what is required of the engine. The manufacturer's

goals may have more to do with emissions and fuel consumption than power output. This is an area of serious engine development, and not something that we, as engine 'modifiers', have much control over.

Finally, consider the mixture ratio and its effect on ignition timing. Weaker mixtures will take longer to burn, so if you run a weaker mixture under cruise conditions or at light throttle, you will need more ignition advance than for a richer mixture.

From all of the preceding you can see that controlling the spark timing is a very important area of tuning. Once we modify an engine away from standard, the spark-timing requirement is going to be different. This is where engine management comes in.

Mechanical advance

With early mechanical advance mechanisms you were limited to advancing with increased rpm. This was achieved with spinning weights in the distributor, which moved out under centrifugal force to a predetermined advance limit. A spring would determine how much the timing advanced at a given rpm, by keeping the weights under control. This gives a straight line of advance on a graph. Basically, the spring load matched the centrifugal force so that advance was controlled by rpm. A development of this was to have two springs of different strengths. The first spring was weaker and allowed advance up to the point where the second spring came into the picture. As the second spring came into play, the two springs worked together to reduce the rate of advance. The big draw-back with this system was that once you had advanced, you couldn't then retard.

Engine load was only sensed mechanically, and it has to be said somewhat clumsily, by a vacuum unit, which advanced the timing by moving the distributor base-plate about. This sliding base-plate was prone to 'wobble' at high rpm due to high frequency vibration periods, and this affected the timing, resulting in what we used to call 'timing scatter'. On race engines the vacuum advance was therefore discarded and the base-plate locked up. This led to many engine modifiers throwing away the vacuum advance unit without really understanding why.

Modification of the mechanical distributor was limited to moving the advance stops and altering the two spring tensions. A high-compression engine generally needs less maximum advance than a standard one, so the full-advance stops needed to be bent or welded-up to limit maximum advance. Initial advance with a modified

Fig. 10.18. Mechanical ignition advance weights in a distributor – (not much) better than nothing.

camshaft needs to be faster than with a stock cam. This means using a weaker initial spring. You need a special distributor-testing machine to set up these parameters – assuming you know what the timing requirement is for the engine. To give someone a basic

engine spec and order a distributor by telephone is patently ridiculous. Bring on the electronics!

Electronic advance

The first step in this direction was replacing the contact-breaker points. The problems with points

Fig. 10.19. The vacuum advance unit is the only way a mechanical system can read engine load. Don't remove it!

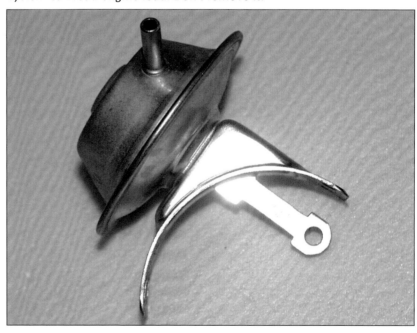

Fig. 10.20. A 'Lumenition' eye replaces the contact breaker points – millions have been sold, and they are totally reliable in the author's experience.

are more mechanical than electrical. The points are opened by a cam, which overcomes the resistance of the spring used to close them. At high speed, when the points come together very quickly they can 'bounce' apart again, because the spring isn't strong enough to overcome the sudden load. This reduces the ignition coil soak time, and can alter the timing if the points haven't settled by the time they are required to open again.

The answer to this problem was the 'contactless' (or 'breakerless') distributor ignition system. An electronic switch with no moving parts replaced the contact breaker points. This switch could be an inductive magnet device, or an optical beam broken by a chopper blade (Lumenition). This was a major step forward, but it also brought its own problems. With the contact breaker system, the vibration from the points rattling against the cam was passed down the distributor shaft to the advance weights. This constant 'shaking' kept the weights free and the advance curve constant.

Once you fit a contactless system, this vibration disappears, and you then introduce some 'stiction' into the advance weights.

This alters the advance curve, so if you carry out a contactless conversion on a contact-breaker distributor, you get slightly retarded timing if the advance weights and springs are not modified. When Lucas introduced their contactless distributor, the timing curve was corrected, but not so in aftermarket kits.

On an engine fitted with a management system, with the ECU already reading engine rpm and load, you then have the ability to put the ignition timing anywhere you want – or more specifically anywhere that the engine wants. This ability to *alter* the ignition timing is the major advantage of mapped ignition, not the *accuracy* of the spark timing. You can advance the ignition with rpm and then retard it again, only to advance it again later. You simply can't do this with a simple mechanical device like a conventional distributor.

For anyone used to dealing with mechanical ignition systems it's hard to grasp the concept that your ECU isn't mechanically linked to the engine. The ECU is nothing more than a very complex timer. If the ECU knows the speed of rotation (rpm) of the crankshaft, and it has a reference point, it can calculate the time taken for the crankshaft to reach a given number of degrees BTDC. The key to understanding this is to think in terms of *time*, not *degrees* of crankshaft rotation. Everything depends on accurate calculation of engine speed.

You start with a trigger reference point well advanced of any required ignition timing needs. If the reference is 90°BTDC, the ECU then holds the spark until the point that it is required, which is dictated by the reference timing in the map. For example, if you want a timing of 30°BTDC then the ECU registers the 90° mark, holds the spark for 60° and then releases it at 30°BTDC. Since a lot of calculations and references are involved in order to arrive at the amount of

time needed for the engine to rotate those 60°, you can only have so much advance available. If you asked for 89°BTDC, then in the time taken for 1° of rotation the ECU can't complete the sums – the system would simply miss the spark altogether, or get it wrong.

The fact that a computer can calculate fast enough to give dead-accurate timing without a physical, mechanical, link is something of a mind-boggling concept if you were brought up on clockwork ignition as I was. Have faith, it works! Engine management gives you total control over the spark timing, and allows you to time the spark so that it occurs whenever the engine wants it, which may depend on any of the previously outlined factors; compression ratio, swirl, tumble, squish and cylinder filling.

Fuel system components

Speed sensor trigger wheels

In order to calculate the engine speed, the ECU needs some sort of reference. Basically that means counting a pulse. If the system knows that two pulses are equal to one revolution, then it can work out the engine speed based on the frequency of pulses produced by the sensor reading from the trigger wheel. The trigger wheel may be mounted in the distributor, or may be fixed directly to the crankshaft.

You normally get two pulses from a four-cylinder engine with a distributor containing four pick-ups. Running at half engine speed the distributor then gives two pulses per engine revolution.

To make things more accurate, if you increase the number of pulses for each revolution of the crankshaft the ECU can keep better track of changes in crankshaft speed. Theoretically, the more pulses the better, but Ford has settled on 36 teeth per revolution, while Bosch has gone for 60 teeth.

Most other manufactures seem to be following Ford's lead and opting for 36 teeth (each tooth on the trigger wheel then represents 10° of crankshaft rotation).

This gives us an accurate picture of crankshaft speed, but not position. In order to work out the piston positions relative to TDC you need a marker point on the trigger wheel. The most common marker is a missing tooth, which will result in a missing pulse. When the ECU sees the pulse missing in a series of pulses, it knows the position of the trigger wheel, and hence the crankshaft. Ford has the tooth missing at 90°BTDC on cylinders 1 and 4, while Bosch use 120°BTDC. Rover, who seem to like making life complicated, started out with 36 teeth, but with two missing tooth sections, 180° apart. They later added two more missing tooth sections, one two teeth away from the first gap, the other three teeth away from the second gap. Not satisfied with that, they then moved all the gaps by another tooth. If you are wondering why they went to all this trouble – so am I! All you need be aware of is that there are many different trigger wheel patterns, and you have to pick the ECU which can handle the configuration you have, or simply change the trigger wheel to suit the ECU.

Throttle bodies

Unlike carburettors, injection throttle bodies are relatively simple devices. All you need is a flap to control the airflow, and a potentiometer on the flap to register movement over the operating range. I have made throttle bodies by cutting up carburettors, machining them, and adding adapters for bell-mouths so that they no longer looked like carburettors. If you aren't concerned about appearances, you can adapt old carburettors very quickly. The catch is that you still need somewhere to put the injector. On my own engine, I turned up aluminium bosses and

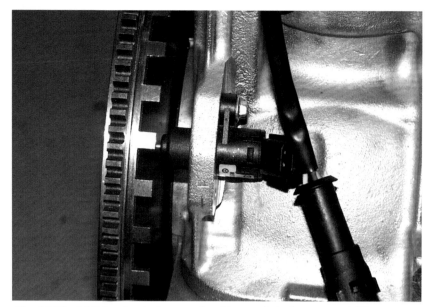

Fig. 10.21. A 36-toothed trigger wheel is crankshaft mounted. The missing tooth relates to the TDC position for the ECU.

Fig. 10.22. Throttle bodies – much less complicated than carbs, and not that difficult to make on a DIY basis.

Fig. 10.23. These bodies are home brewed – they may not look immaculate, but they work just as well as the manufacturers' offerings.

Fig. 10.24. If you make your own bodies you can put the injector boss in the inlet manifold. This boss has been welded into place.

welded these into the inlet manifold.

Life is a lot easier if you buy purpose-made throttle bodies, which contain the injector and come complete with fuel rail and fitting clips. Most professional throttle bodies use butterfly throttle-plates, but not all. Slide throttles were popular at one time, but they have several disadvantages (the least one not being the price). With a slide throttle you can get sticking under high engine vacuum conditions, such as on overrun when the vacuum pulls the slide against its runners. Ball-bearing systems do help, but you still have the slide opening the throttle from one side of the induction port. On four-valve engines this is a distinct disadvantage, when ideally you want to expose both inlet valves at the same time.

Barrel throttles, whereby two counter-rotating barrels open from the centre of the body, leave the induction totally clear on full throttle, but you can get fuel puddles building up against the bottom roller on less than full throttle if the injector is upstream of the throttle. If you run double injectors, set up as described in the

'Fuelling theory' section, you will not have any problems. However, barrel throttles are very expensive and normally have to be custom made for a specific engine.

Considering their simplicity, butterfly bodies work extremely well, as long as they are matched correctly to the engine. There are several considerations to be taken

into account when selecting the bore size of the bodies. First off, most people go for too big a body. We are all greedy by nature, and if big is good then bigger must be better – not so.

Although we are injecting fuel into the inlet system, we still need some air speed to carry that fuel into the engine. Too large a body

Fig. 10.25. Barrel throttle bodies offer no resistance to airflow when fully open, and they are theoretically more efficient than butterfly types.

reduces air speed and leads to fuel drop-out – exactly the same problem as we get in a carburettor. The situation isn't helped when throttle body manufacturers copy their sizes from carburettors, 40/45/48/50mm are exactly as you find in Weber carburettors. The reason for this is to enable you to match the throttle bodies to carburettor inlet manifolds – sensible marketing.

The problem with this sizing is that people either duplicate their carburettor size, or go one larger, thinking that injection isn't so sensitive on bore size. But carburettors have a restriction called a 'venturi', which reduces the bore of the inlet. A 40mm carburettor may well only house a 30mm hole. The 40mm throttle body has a 40mm hole right through it.

Next consider your mapping system. You have a throttle potentiometer to register throttle opening. With a large-bore body, the initial opening gives a lot more intake area than you get with a smaller body. True, you can close up load sites, but it makes it very difficult to map. At low engine speeds you will find that you get full power on less than full throttle, and further opening (increasing load) just drops the power away, as blow-back starts to take place. Effectively, you waste half your map sites at low rpm and larger load positions.

Fig. 10.26. The throttle potentiometer has to be a good fit on the throttle body spindle, any slack will play havoc with the mapping.

By using a smaller body, you get smoother progression on initial opening, more control over the mapping, better fuel consumption and reduced hydrocarbon emissions – because the higher air speed carries more fuel into the engine. Less drop-out means less raw fuel going into the chamber, less waste and cleaner burning. Having selected the right bore size for your body, you then need to select the right length.

Injectors

Total fuel flow will depend on base fuel-line pressure and the flow rate of the injector. Most amateur engine builders select overly large injectors. Sometimes this is a result of unrealistic power expectations, and sometimes the result of bad advice. Ideally you want the injectors to operate between 20% and 80% of the available pulse-width time (for a given rpm). If looking for a double injector set-up, you can obviously fit injectors with lower flow because you have two of them to supply maximum fuelling. This also gives you more accurate fuel metering at light loads, because the single injector is operating closer to maximum capacity.

Individual injector flow can be measured on a test rig, and this is worth doing if you choose to buy used injectors. Top-running teams have sets of injectors matched for flow, but this is only worth the trouble if you have very good airflow management in the engine. If different cylinders have different airflow ability, then the fuelling requirement will not be the same for every cylinder.

The fuel flow pattern from the injectors can be a cone or a diffused spray. You can inspect the pattern on the flow test rig, but

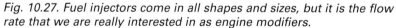

Fig. 10.27. Fuel injectors come in all shapes and sizes, but it is the flow rate that we are really interested in as engine modifiers.

Fig. 10.28. Most injectors are top-feed, like this one.

Fig. 10.29. The bottom-feed injector allows a constant flow of fuel past the body, helping to keep the injector cool.

Fig. 10.30. This injector has four bleed holes allowing air to enter the fuel outlet area aiding mixture presentation to the engine.

when the injectors are fitted to the engine, under high vacuum conditions the shape of the spray does change, beautiful cone shapes often narrowing into a pencil line. This does not apply when you fit the injector outside the intake system, as with the outer injectors on a double-injector set-up. I have seen wide cone-angle injectors that spray their fuel at such a wide angle that it impinges on the side of the trumpet and forms a wet wall. This does not reach the engine in time to burn with the fuel from the first injector. The engine then runs very weak and misfires. Watch out for this if fitting upper and lower injectors using second-hand parts.

Most injectors are top-feed, in that the fuel enters the top of the injector and waits for the injector to open. Side, or bottom-feed injectors have a through-flow of fuel, which helps to keep the fuel cool. Remember that colder fuel will take more heat from the air, increasing the air density, and therefore giving better power.

Bottom-feed injectors normally come as part of a fuel rail assembly, and are more difficult to engineer into an alternative application, although I have used Ford Zetec bottom-feed injectors in a CVH application. At the time of writing, some OE engine

manufacturers are looking at an injector that bleeds air into the spray cone to improve mixture presentation, but I have no data or details as yet.

The resistance of injectors should always be measured before installation. Very early electronic injection systems used low impedance coils with a resistance of about 3 ohms. The idea was to get the current flowing very quickly so that the injector opened at a faster rate. Later systems use injectors with a resistance of about 15 or 16 ohms, and you cannot mix the two. Some ECU systems can cope with either type of injector, but others need a resistor in the earth line to prevent the injector driver from overheating.

Fuel rail and fuel pressure regulator

When making up a fuel rail you do need to consider some sort of take-off for checking the base fuel-line pressure of the fuel pressure regulator. I have found that a lot of people fit adjustable regulators, but never check or set the pressure. Basically the fuel pump can deliver a lot more pressure than the system requires. The job of the regulator is to keep the pressure constant, so that each injector pulse delivers the same amount of

fuel. Small changes in base fuel-line pressure will give quite substantial changes in fuel delivery from a given injector.

A pressure regulator is basically a spring-loaded diaphragm which bypasses fuel to the return line when a set spring pressure is exceeded. You can adjust the pressure of the spring via a plunger and locking nut on purpose-made adjustable regulators. On standard regulators you can often gain small increases in pressure by squeezing the regulator in a clamp. This crushes the body down and increases the spring tension. Note that this is a one-way street.

The pressure regulator vacuum connection to the inlet manifold has nothing to do with snap throttle response or engine acceleration on the standard system. The idea is that additional fuel will naturally be drawn from the injector when the manifold is under vacuum (idle condition), compared to when there is no vacuum present (full throttle). By linking the base fuel-line pressure to the manifold vacuum, you ensure that the system always operates under a constant condition relative to manifold pressure. With competition engines running separate throttle bodies, most people leave this vacuum pipe disconnected. If you

Fig. 10.31. The adjustable pressure regulator allows the base line pressure to be easily adjusted. Set it before you start work.

Fig. 10.32. A standard pressure regulator can have its pressure increased by squeezing it in the vice to compress the internal spring.

Fuel filters

are mapping a competition engine from scratch, it makes no practical difference. There is nothing wrong with the pressure regulator supplied with standard injection systems. Generally they are small, light and reliable. Wherever possible I use stock regulators for the above reasons. I work on the principle that if it isn't broke, then I don't fix it! Most standard regulators can be made into adjustable ones by welding or brazing a nut on top of the regulator body and using a bolt and washer to act on the internal spring. If you have some fabrication skills and suitable

equipment, this makes more sense than buying a large cast-alloy regulator that takes up more room and increases overall weight.

Having the ability to quickly alter base fuel-line pressure can be very useful, but equally you need to be able to quickly connect a pressure gauge. This needs to be a gauge capable of measuring in the 0 to 10 bar range. A lot of fuel rails are equipped with a standard pressure gauge take-off valve, and you can buy gauges with adapters to link straight into these, otherwise it's a case of finding the right fittings to link into the *feed* side of the system, *not* the return.

You must have a fuel filter in the supply line to the pump. The pump needs protecting from dirt that could damage it, so a filter needs to go between the pump pick-up and the pump itself. Injectors have very fine calibrated holes, so any dirt getting into them could quickly turn them into scrap. For this reason you must use a very fine filter prior to fuel delivery to the injectors.

It's possible to buy 'competition' type filters in beautiful anodised aluminium cylinders, but they are not of throw-away design, and have to be cleaned by changing the internal element. Personally I find

Fig. 10.33. The 'race' fuel filter is said to have massive flow capability but, probably more importantly, it looks very fast.

Fig. 10.34. Stock fuel filters will have enough flow reserve for most modified engines. Change them at regular intervals, they are not fit-and-forget items.

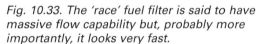

the stock manufacturer's filters lighter and simpler to use. Flow rates are not normally a problem, especially if you choose a filter from a car with a similar power output to your own engine's predicted power.

When installing the filter, try to put it in a place where you will not just forget all about it! Out of sight tends to become out of mind. The filter should be changed every year on a competition car, which does more standing around than anything else.

Fuel pumps and fuel lines

Fuel injection systems operate with base fuel-line pressures anywhere between 2.5 and 5 bar. That's 37 to 74psi. A typical carburettor needs a pressure of 3 to 5psi to supply fuel to the float chamber. *Do not use carburettor hose for injection systems!* Time and time again you see bulging fuel hoses on new installations. Just because a length of hose has a fancy stainless steel braided wrap, it doesn't mean it's a strong hose. You must use high-pressure fuel hose for all flexible connections on a fuel injection system. Ideally, run as much of the system in solid pipe as you can, usually the internal bore will be larger than a flexible hose, and you will save vast sums of money, which can be spent elsewhere on the car. Professional race installations use threaded fittings at all joints, while car manu-facturers use hoses and clips. There's nothing wrong with hoses and clips as long as they are up to the job.

Up until a few years ago fuel pumps were all mounted outside the fuel tank, and in-line. Now most car manufacturers are fitting pumps inside the fuel tank, with the pump sitting on the bottom of the fuel tank. For a DIY installation, external pumps are a lot easier to fit, and there is no practical technical reason for fitting a submerged pump. What really

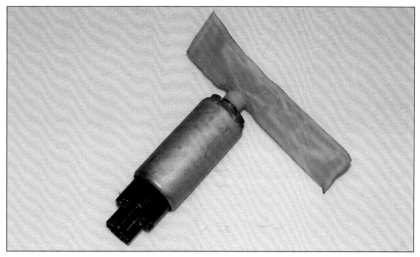

Fig. 10.35. The latest generation of fuel pumps sit inside the fuel tank – less plumbing more difficult to access.

matters is the design of the fuel pick-up inside the tank.

Unlike the pump in a carburettor fuel system, the pump in an injection system is moving a lot of fuel about the system. One small hick-up in the fuel supply will result in a weak-mixture flat-spot. Unlike the carburettor, an injection system has no float chamber to act as a reserve if fuel surges away from the pick-up during cornering. The

fuel supply to the pressure regulator must be constant. The pick-up design must include baffles to keep the fuel around the pick-up pipe at all times. OE manufacturers take a lot of trouble to get this right. If you rob parts from an injected model to convert a carburettor one, rob the fuel tank too!

One very effective solution to the problem of fuel surge on injected engines is to run a swirl

Fig. 10.36. The external pump is easier to fit and much easier to change if you do get a problem. Note the fuel filter mounted in-line with the pump.

pot. This term has been borrowed from the cooling system. In fact the swirl pot is nothing more than a reserve tank. The main tank carries the bulk of the fuel, and a low-pressure carburettor pump lifts the fuel to the swirl pot. From there a high-pressure injection pump supplies the fuel rail and pressure regulator, with the return going to the swirl pot. It's a mini fuel tank supplied by a large reserve one. Fuel surge at the main tank only causes a drop in level at the swirl pot, which recovers when the main system comes back on line.

Alternatives to engine mapping

Chip tuning and chip conversions

I used this 'chip' term simply because it is in common usage, you are not tuning the chip, converting it, or doing anything else to it! When cars with electronic-injection engines first appeared, a big market sprang up for ECUs with altered map settings in the memory. These units were aimed at turbo engines, where the ECU controlled the boost levels. By altering the settings in the map, you could increase the boost, and so increase the power level.

For a really wild 'conversion' you could also remove the rev limiter, and some people made a lot of money from destroying otherwise perfectly sound engines. As things got more sophisticated, these modified maps got more complex, and rather than just removing limits, they were effectively re-mapped. Once the notion of 'chip tuning' was embedded in young and impressionable minds, the term took on an almost mythical meaning. Suddenly you could buy a chip for any car – turbo or normally aspirated.

A chip conversion just means fitting a memory chip with altered map settings. Prior to the electronic era, nobody got that

Fig. 10.37. The standard ECU has all the maps in memory, but you can't manipulate them.

excited about fitting a bigger main jet and moving the ignition timing. Before the manufacturer put in the original settings, they spent something like two years of research arriving at them. But this gave the engine an average setting for an average engine. Also, some weak mixture areas were built in for fuel economy or emissions reasons. Adding more fuel and some spark advance sometimes gives more power, but I have never understood how one set of modified parameters was supposed to work for all 'average' engines from the same vehicle model range.

Logic dictates that if you can sometimes get a gain in perform-

ance by fine-tuning the ECU to the actual engine, rather than an average one, then you need to do just that when chip tuning. This has now become known as the 'bespoke chip'. Just like a visit to your bespoke tailor, it is quite an expensive experience.

Signal modifiers (piggy-back ECUs)

Mention has to be made of 'piggy-back' ECUs. These are devices, which interrupt the signals going into the standard ECU, and replace them with false signals. In the early days people would solder a resistor into the coolant temperature signal wire to tell the

ECU that the engine was a little colder than it actually was. This fooled the ECU into providing additional fuel.

Piggy-back ECUs are a more sophisticated development of the same theory. You either interrupt the signals *to* the ECU, or the ones coming *from* it. By doing this, you can wrest control of the engine from the original management system, while still making the original system do all the complicated work.

A map from a piggy-back ECU will not look like a normal map. Rather, it will be a map containing plus and minus numbers. These are the figures that must be added to, or subtracted from, the original map settings to arrive at what the engine is actually seeing. As with all things, there are limitations. The addition of extra fuel is a classic example.

Because you are only giving the existing ECU false information, it can't in the end supply more fuel than it had in its memory to start with. Most standard cars use an airflow meter of some description. If you interrupt the signal wire from the ECU to increase fuelling, the brain will eventually figure out that there can't possibly be that much air going into the engine – you will have gone outside the limit of its original mapping parameter. As long as you stay within the original parameter limit, and there is always some leeway built into any system, you don't run into problems.

If you do run out of fuel, you have to take fairly drastic measures. You can increase the base fuel-line pressure, but this will result in more fuel going in everywhere. Then you have to go back into the modifying maps and

Fig. 10.38. This Unichip device allows you to alter the input signal and fool the original ECU into giving a different value from the base map.

remove fuel from the whole system, except at the point where you had originally run out. This practically means re-mapping the whole engine.

If you fit a modified camshaft, or modify the engine in a way that the airflow meter doesn't like (big pulses can confuse the metering), you can't easily adjust the ECU using false signals to compensate. What you can do is look at moving to a throttle-position-based map, which is really starting from scratch as you would be with any programmable ECU.

Another problem when running a highly modified engine with a piggy-back ECU is the rev limiter. You can't really fool the ECU on engine revs. If you start replacing the speed signal with a false signal, the ECU will start moving to that section of the map for fuel and ignition settings. You are pretty

much stuck with the stock rev limiter, unless you can have this removed at source (from within the main ECU).

What piggy-back ECUs *are* very good at is what they were designed for; they give you a means of fine-tuning a standard engine. If you compare the cost of an add-on ECU, like the Dastek Unichip, against a conventional modified ECU, then you would have to pick the Unichip every time – even though you have to allow a little extra cost for the setting-up time. If you change your car, you can also transfer this chip to another car with the same input system.

One point I would make about modified road cars is that you must inform your insurance company. If you have a bad accident, and the insurance assessor finds a modified ECU, it could mean that your insurance is invalid.

Chapter 11
Component installation

Introduction

It isn't within the scope of this book to cover detailed installation on any one system. However, some general points wouldn't go amiss. First off, READ THE MANUAL! In my experience, so many people start wiring up and powering up, without so much as looking at the installation instructions. Only after they have blown the ECU do they find they have wired up the injector drivers incorrectly.

Next, having read the manual, take some notice of what it is telling you. If the book says connect two major earth wires direct to the battery, don't connect them to the chassis – even if you have resistance checked the path. If the book says keep certain wires apart, or away from HT leads, don't twist them together to make a neat looking job. Check all connections and make sure they are mechanically safe. Wires dangling unsupported from the throttle pot, perhaps with a heavy plug on the end, will fatigue and break after a period of time. A cable tie will ensure they last a lifetime.

ECU

Basically, installing an ECU is a question of wiring it into the car. Some systems come with completed looms which you simply plug in, others have nothing more than a wiring diagram. The best place to fit the ECU will depend on the layout of the car, but the passenger footwell is nice and dry, and that's where most manufacturers fit their original-equipment system ECUs.

Throttle body and throttle potentiometer

Fitting throttle bodies is not like fitting carburettors. You have no need of flexible mounts for a start, since you have no float chamber to be disturbed by engine vibration. What you do still need is a decent throttle linkage and a reliable system for mounting the throttle potentiometer.

Starting with the throttle linkage, the first requirement is that you do get full throttle movement. This sounds obvious, but it's more important with injection systems than carburettors. On the end of the throttle body you will have a throttle potentiometer (throttle pot). This tells the ECU how far open the throttle is. Most systems have an automatic calibration for range in their software. If the throttles only move over 75% of their travel, you then align the throttle pot to cover that range, which the pot takes to be 100% of the available movement. So many people get half-way through mapping an engine, only to find that full throttle isn't available. Adjusting the linkage to get full travel then means re-alignment of the pot, and all your previous mapping is out of the window!

Professional throttle bodies will have the industry standard 8mm spindle with a 'D' drive on the end.

Fig. 11.1. Check for full throttle before you start work.

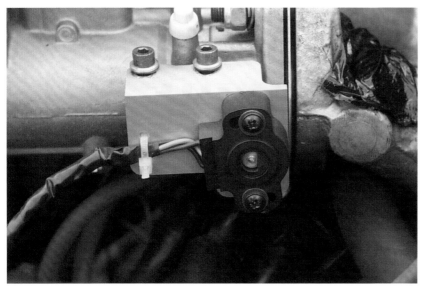

Fig. 11.2. For three-dimensional mapping of the ignition, even carbs need a throttle pot added to their butterfly spindle.

Automotive throttle pots fit straight over this 'D', and the spring pretension in the pot ensures you never get free play between the spindle and the pot. If you make up your own linkage or pot drive, take a lot of trouble to ensure there is no free play in the linkage. If there is, you will be mapping for the rest of your life, chasing seemingly random alterations in the fuel map settings. Don't say that you weren't warned!

When installing the pot, you need to ensure that it is a little way off its zero setting. Since you won't know the spindle/butterfly idle position at this stage, you need to allow for some additional closing of the pot. If the pot is already fully closed and you shut the throttles down some more, at best that movement won't be recorded. At worst you will damage the pot. When wiring the pot, make sure the wires are supported. Vibration can cause the wires to fracture, and once that happens, the ECU will not receive any load reading. Some ECUs require a minimum pot number as the start of their working range. Check the installation manual on this point. It's vital that you get this right before you start mapping. So many people have mapping problems due to a simple mechanical error with installation, which they *always* mistake for an electronics problem. The throttle pot is the major sensor for a competition management system, and as the computer boys say: 'rubbish in = rubbish out'.

Fig. 11.3. Unsupported wires can break due to vibration – the most common cause of 'ECU' problems is poor electrical connections. Fit brackets or clips to support long wire runs.

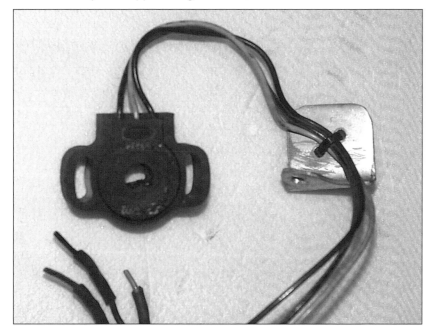

Ignition amplifiers

The ignition amplifier (ignition amp) is a classic example of a component which can fail due to not reading the instructions. Any external amplifier will get hot. The manufacturers fit their amps on a heat sink, and supply a heat conducting jelly to be used at the junction of amp and heat sink. I've seen people take the amp off a car and 'clean up' the area before refitting. That jelly was there for a reason, if the amp overheats it fails – an instant engine stopper!

On new installations, it's common on kit cars for people to fit the amps straight onto the bulkhead. This is usually glassfibre, and glassfibre isn't known for its heat-conducting ability. Better still, I've seen a mounting plate made from very 'fast' carbon-fibre, which is an even better insulator than glassfibre. Please use aluminium for amplifier installation, polish it if you must, but make sure it keeps the amp cool.

Speed sensors

Finally, a word on speed sensors. There are several different types of speed sensor, and the type of

Fig. 11.5. This is not grease! Heat soak jelly aids the transfer of heat from the amplifier to the surrounding heat sink.

Fig. 11.4. A generous heat sink will stop the ignition amp overheating when it is current limiting – this occurs mainly during idle conditions.

sensor used depends on the engine type. Distributor systems generally use either optical, hall-effect or magnetic-reluctance sensors. Make sure that the sensor provides the right type of signal for the ECU to pick up. Some systems offer alternatives, and you may need to use a different loom or connections depending on the speed signal type.

Rotor arm alignment is one of the biggest headaches you are likely to come across with distributor-based management systems. When you lock up the

distributor advance weights, the rotor arm remains in a fixed position at all times. With the ECU giving you the ability to run a lot of ignition advance on light throttle, you can easily get to the stage where the spark arrives before the rotor arm has aligned with the correct HT lead. Cross-firing is the result and the engine bangs and back-fires quite dramatically.

The problem comes about because you need to rotate the distributor body to give the required reference for the trigger system. 66° BTDC is a common

setting. If the distributor was from an ECU-driven system, you will not have a problem. However, for a system converted from bob-weights, this will be way in advance of normal running, and the rotor arm will almost certainly be pointing in the wrong direction when there is a lot of advance in the map. The fix is relatively simple.

The distributor needs a given reference so that the timing that the ECU thinks it is providing is the timing that you are getting at the engine. If the distributor is advanced or retarded, the numbers in the map will be meaningless because the ECU's reference start point is wrong. You can check the

Fig. 11.6. Incorrect rotor arm positioning can cause the spark to jump to the wrong terminal – this is known as 'cross-firing'.

Fig. 11.7. Checking the ignition timing with a timing light.

alignment with a timing light. If the actual timing on the crankshaft marks is different from the timing in the ECU map, you will need to move the distributor until the two readings coincide.

Once you have set the position of the distributor body to give the correct reference, turn the crankshaft so that number one piston is rising on its compression stroke, then position the piston at TDC. Note the position of the rotor arm. Most rotor arms are located by a slot in the drive spindle. Lift the arm and rotate it to point at one of the HT pick-ups in the distributor cap, so that the trailing edge of the arm is just *past* the pick-up. Mark the position of the arm on the drive spindle, and cut a new slot in the spindle so that the rotor arm now points to the pick-up in the distributor cap as described previously. Use this new pick-up as number one, and move the HT leads accordingly. You can paint-mark the new position so that no confusion arises if the rotor arm is removed at any time.

Using a toothed wheel is an option for distributorless operation. You can buy wheels from Ford and Vauxhall which can be adapted to your own engine.

Fig. 11.8. The rotor arm can be re-positioned so that it lines up as the ignition advances, simply cut a second slot in the spindle.

The Ford wheel (Part No 88WM6K339AB) has 36–1 tooth pattern, while the Vauxhall wheel has 60–2. Basically, if you are going to mount either wheel on your crankshaft, you start by deciding where the sensor is going to sit. Once you have decided on the sensor position (probably dictated by the most convenient bracket location), you then need to position the crankshaft to the reference setting. Ford use a reference of 90° BTDC on cylinders one and four, while Vauxhall (Bosch) use 120° BTDC. Basically, the first tooth after the gap in the timing wheel needs to pass the sensor when the crankshaft is positioned at the given reference setting.

With the trigger wheel positioned so that the first tooth after the gap is aligned with the sensor pick-up, fix the trigger wheel to the crankshaft in this position.

It may sound complicated, but if you follow the above sequence you will not get it wrong. The most

Fig. 11.9. An inexpensive 36–1 toothed wheel can be sourced from the Ford parts bin.

Fig. 11.10. The pick-up sensor has to be positioned correctly relative to TDC. With the 36–1 wheel this is 90°BTDC firing on cylinder Nos 1 and 4.

common mistakes are to set the engine and fix the sensor wheel, then put the sensor in the wrong place, or to set the engine to the right position, but on the wrong cylinders. Remember that the sensor wheel can be in any position relative to the crankshaft, as long as the first tooth after the gap passes the sensor at the right time.

If you are not too confident of you sensor positioning, make the bracket adjustable so that you can fine-tune it once you have the engine running. Some ECU systems allow you to put in an offset via the software, so that slight misalignment can be catered for.

If you opt for the Ford sensor wheel mentioned previously (it's the cheapest option), be aware that the teeth are not terribly strong. This means that if you continually rev to 7500rpm, or more, the teeth will probably bend outwards under centrifugal force and wipe out the sensor! As a precaution, you can shorten the teeth by a couple of millimetres to reduce their tendency to bend.

Interference

When electricity flows through a conductor it creates a magnetic field. Alternatively, if you pass a magnetic field through a conductor you get a flow of electricity. This is the first, most basic, principle of

Fig. 11.11. Suppressed HT leads are essential for an engine fitted with any electronic devices, especially management systems.

electronics, but so many people forget all about it when installing an engine-management system. What we are talking about here is interference caused by magnetic waves inducting a current into a wire – current that shouldn't be there. Underbonnet electronic 'noise' can cause an ECU to cut dead, misfire, or generally get very confused. It isn't the ECU at fault, you are telling the system lies by feeding false information into the ECU. Most of the noise under the bonnet comes from the ignition HT circuit. Non-suppressed HT leads are a complete non-starter for engine-management systems. The best leads have additional suppression above the level found in normal carbon string leads.

Next, consider the spark plugs. All the latest production engines run sophisticated engine-management systems. They also all run with 'resistor'-type spark plugs. Fit non-resistor plugs to a modern engine and it will simply stop playing. Misfires, engine cuts and spit-backs after a service can,

Fig. 11.12. Resistor spark plugs are the answer to 90% of interference problems.

Fig. 11.13. Often a misfire will be due to something as simple as an HT leak – often due to damaged or corroded connections like the one on the right!

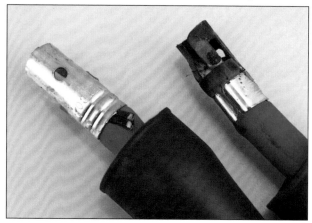

in many cases, be tracked down to someone not fitting resistor-type spark plugs. The introduction of resistor leads has been the biggest single factor in cutting down radiated electronic noise emissions on production cars to an acceptable level.

The main areas for picking up interference are the signal wires going into the ECU. The speed sensor wiring is the most important, followed by the throttle pot wires. The first consideration is routing. You do not want any signal wires running close to ignition

Fig. 11.14. Run your signal wire too close to an electrical field (such as the ignition coil), and you will get interference.

Fig. 11.15. A good timing light is essential when initially setting up.

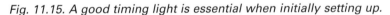

coils and HT leads if it can be avoided. The next consideration is shielding. You can buy shielded wire, which is basically normal wiring surrounded by a braid of copper. You connect the copper shielding braid to earth by twisting it up and soldering an earth tag to it. The idea of shielded wire is that any magnetic interference passing through the outer plastic cover is picked up by the braid, and shunted to earth before it can reach the signal wires located underneath the braid. The essential thing about using shielded wire is that you have to remember to earth the braid! I don't know how many times I have come across neat installations using shielded wire, which isn't actually doing anything except looking the part.

Hall-effect or square wave signals (three wire) are the cleanest signals as far as the ECU is concerned, and less prone to interference. The inductive or reluctor triggers (two wire) are the more problematic. One of the problems concerns connecting the sensor up with the wires reversed. With most ECUs the engine will still run, but the signal will be triggering from the wrong edge of the signal wave. The signal will effectively move around depending on rpm, and the timing will vary away from the map setting. You can also get misfiring with increased engine rpm.

The only way to track this condition is with a timing light, referenced against the interpolated map timing. In other words, checking that what you are getting is what the computer thinks it is putting out.

If the ECU is equipped with a rev limiter and a shift light, these can give you a good indication of interference in the speed signal wiring. When a pulse appears in the line close to the genuine signal pulse, the ECU sees this as high rpm, and if this exceeds the rev limit or shift-light setting, then the engine misfires (rev limiter coming in) and the shift light flashes.

Chapter 12

Engine mapping

Mapping aids

If you try to map an engine by the seat of your pants, you are quickly going to get yourself into trouble. In an ideal world, you need a gas analyser, a wide-range lambda mixture reader, and a dynamometer to do a 100% job. In the real world you can make do with less.

In order to optimise the ignition timing, you can't really do without a rolling road. On the other hand, ignition isn't hard to get close just by putting in sensible, or known values. If the engine pinks under test, you can note the map site and back off the timing at this point. However, to get it absolutely right, you need to measure the power output, holding the speed/load site and adjusting the timing for maximum power. There's no other way to do it.

The fuelling is a different story. The gas analyser is a useful tool,

Fig. 12.1. The gas analyser is really too slow for serious mapping, but it's essential for passing the MoT test.

but it isn't very good for mapping. The time delay between sampling and reading is too long to safely allow an engine to be held under load, whilst making a change and waiting for the result. However, for setting the idle fuelling it is essential to have a four-gas analyser if you want to pass any sort of government emission test.

The lambda mixture reader is a much more useful tool. For accuracy you should kit yourself out with a wide-range reading lambda sensor and the hardware to read from it. This will include corrections for exhaust gas temperature amongst other things. Prices start at around £4000 sterling – a lot more than any amateur would want to pay.

The mixture reader that links to a standard lambda sensor is a different story. These cost less than £200, and they give you a good indication of when the mixture is chemically correct – stoichiometric

Fig. 12.2. A lambda mixture reader will reduce mapping time considerably, getting you into the right area very quickly.

as the engineers say. It's only when you stray from this central area of the range of the sensor that the mixture reading becomes less accurate. Even so, although these readers may not be accurate enough for factory calibrations, they certainly work well enough for DIY mapping. Some ECUs contain drivers and software to display a lambda value, either as a raw number, or often as a coloured bar graph.

If money is really tight, you can use a half-decent voltmeter wired direct to the lambda sensor. The mixture is stoichiometric when you are reading 0.5 volts, and the reading will swing from 0.2 volts when rich, to 0.8 volts when weak.

Armed with a mixture reader, it is theoretically possible to map an engine by driving the car on the road or track – in reality it's very difficult to do. The problem is that you can't hold a speed site. You can apply throttle, but as you do so the engine accelerates along the speed sites. The only way to avoid this is to left-foot brake the car, and at big throttle openings you are going to set the brakes on fire holding the car back. Speaking from personal experience, I was almost arrested

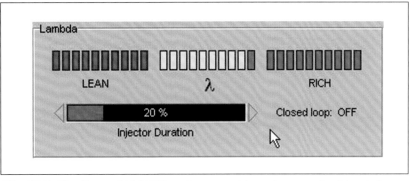

Fig. 12.3. The Emerald M3DK system provides a bar graph of lambda value on screen.

trying to map a production racer on the public highway. The car wasn't actually going that fast, but on full throttle, with the brakes hard on, it certainly sounded like it was. The real answer is a rolling road.

Rolling road vs dynamometer cell for mapping

I am a big fan of engine dynamometers. You can read power directly from the flywheel, and you can hold load all day without boiling the engine. Engine dynamometers are a great development tool. If you want to run the engine prior to installation,

dial in the cam and sort out the intake and exhaust lengths, the dyno cell is the place to be. But you often find people trying to use the engine dyno to map their engine. The belief is that an engine dyno is more accurate than a rolling road. However, you can get big problems using an engine dyno for mapping if the operator runs a 'dyno cell' exhaust and no silencers. I honestly believe that if you can't use the car's exhaust and silencer in the cell, with fitted lengths exactly as they are on the car, then it's a waste of time. Once you take the engine off the dyno and put it in the car, all the parameters will change.

Fig. 12.4. A rolling road is ideal for setting up, but less useful for engine development.

Fig. 12.5. The dyno cell can be used for mapping – provided you have the engine fitted out as it will be installed in the car. Here, the exhaust system is not the one to be fitted in the car.

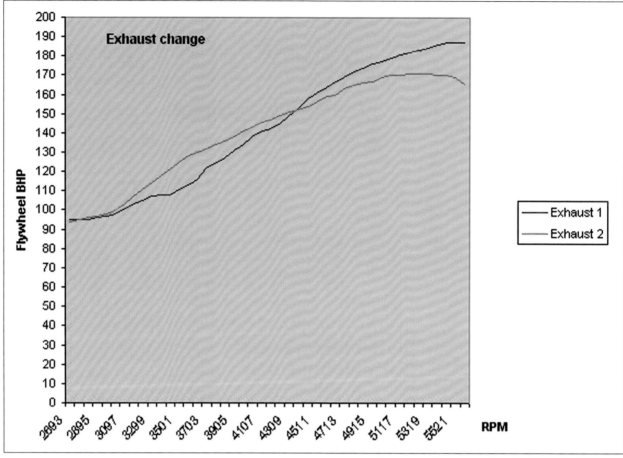

Fig. 12.6. The exhaust system makes a big difference to the shape of the power curve. This is the curve for a Proton National saloon car.

Fig. 12.7. The rolling-road absorption unit should be of the closed-loop eddy-current type, as shown here, for rapid mapping.

Don't kid yourself that a different exhaust type or length isn't going to make much difference. I've seen an engine producing 160bhp jump to 180bhp just by changing the exhaust pipe diameter, let alone the length. The rolling road with the car in race-ready trim is the place to do your final mapping. A lot of people argue that rolling roads are inaccurate, and this used to be true. Old water-brake rolling roads only measured the power at the wheels, and it took forever to stabilise an rpm site. By the time you had the right speed and load point, the engine had all but melted. The power also appeared to be constantly changing.

When you hold an engine under load on the rollers, the tyres heat up. The more load, the greater the heat generated by the rolling resistance in the tyres. The hotter

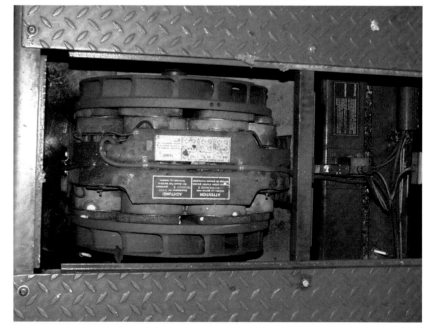

the tyres get, the more the pressure in the tyre goes up. This in turn reduces the rolling resistance. It's a vicious circle that makes accurate power reading all but impossible. With the appearance of electric-brake, eddy-current rolling roads all that changed.

With an electric brake, you can measure power at a predetermined acceleration rate. You can allow the engine to accelerate at exactly the same rate, time and time again. If you start with the same engine temperature each time, you get real repeatability. However, the real breakthrough came with measuring run-down resistance.

The rolling road works by measuring the torque on an arm, which is pressing on an electronic load cell. If you make the cell so

Fig. 12.8. The electronic load cell feeds back the torque which is used to calculate bhp at the wheels.

Fig. 12.9. The run-down measures losses and adds them to the power at the wheels to give a 'simulated' flywheel figure. Often depressingly accurate!

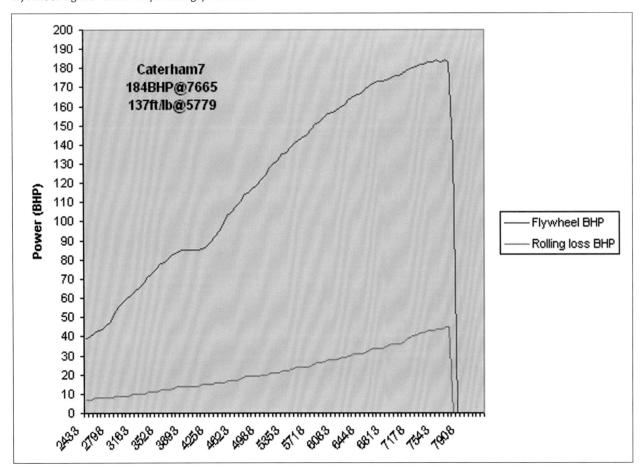

that it can read in two directions, you can knock the car out of gear and measure the torque on the overrun. With the inertia of the rollers a known factor, you can measure the rolling resistance very accurately – and it's repeatable.

Run the car up, knock it out of gear, and the software in the computer reads the rolling resistance. On my Sun RAM X11, I can record power curves that sit one on top of the other, time and again – as long as the engine is stable. Some engines are very sensitive to coolant temperature, and you will get changes with subsequent runs. I reckon to work within one bhp with a stable engine, and you can pick-up, lose and then recover, one bhp with regularity.

Road and track testing

After the rolling road or dyno set up, you need to test under actual driving conditions. You often find

Fig. 12.10. Road testing is essential after a setting-up session. Not everything shows up on the rolling road.

things in the real world that never show up in the test environment. One example is that when setting up, you never go into an overrun condition for more than a few seconds. But when driving, you are on overrun a lot of the time – especially when braking from top

Fig. 12.11. Road testing should be carried out on a quiet, traffic-free road.

speed for a hairpin bend. You may find that on the overrun you are getting a lot of explosions in the exhaust, with flames exiting the tailpipe. It looks dramatic, and discourages tail-gating, but it can also damage silencer internals. There's a very easy fix.

What is happening is that you have the mixture too weak on high rpm/light load sites. The weak mixture passes through the engine, and misses the spark. The fuel builds up in the exhaust until it is rich enough to explode, triggered by the heat in the silencer. Richen up the mixture across the light-throttle range, and the explosions disappear. The better method is to use the overrun fuel cut-off in the software. Some people will tell you that using the overrun cut-off results in a hesitation when you go back on the throttle. These people pay good money to have these overrun cut-off systems removed from stock ECUs. I've never found it a problem, and I doubt that you will.

During testing you can check the acceleration fuelling. If there are still flat spots present, you can increase the compensation and try it again. With a lap-top computer, it's an easy job to make small changes at the track. If there are no flat spots, check your mirror. Can you see any tell-tale signs of black smoke? If so, you can then reduce acceleration fuelling until you lose the smoke.

If possible, cut the engine from high speed, and check the spark plug colour. Bearing in mind that you are checking the temperature of the plug, you can confirm that the grade is correct, since you already know the mixture is correct for maximum power. You can also check the mixture distribution by comparing plugs. With big V8 engines, fuel distribution can be a pain, but you can also get problems on four-cylinder engines that run plenum chambers, or on any system without individual inlets for each port. It may be possible to compensate by swapping injectors about. If the

injectors are not a matched set, you can sometimes get variations that you can utilise to offset uneven airflow. Track testing can be more effective here than dyno testing.

Testing in the rain can be very revealing for a mapped engine. All that power that you worked so hard to find on the dyno can be an embarrassment if the sudden power surge, as the engine comes on cam, causes massive wheel-spin. You may find that lap times improve in the wet if you retard the ignition at the point where torque initially climbs. This will soften the hit as the power comes in, and will help to retain traction. You only need to modify the full-load site, and perhaps the one above it. Save the map as under different name, and remember to put the original map back for racing in the dry.

Some management systems now incorporate a 'power reducer' button. This allows you to retard the whole map by a given amount at the press of a button. Some drivers use this to soften power delivery when getting off the line. Track testing is the time to find out how much retard you need.

With full control over the fuel and ignition settings, there is no end of tricks that you can put into a system. How many of them are of real practical benefit is difficult to say. Sometimes software engineers put in 'beneficial' features, which answer a question that nobody has asked. Track testing is the only way to dial in and evaluate such trickery. If it really works, the race organisers will probably ban it!

Initial start-up and idling

Any system that you buy will be supplied with a base map of sorts for fuelling, and probably ignition. If you are very lucky it will be a map from an identical engine (highly unlikely) and you can install it and drive away. This never happens in the real world.

Fig. 12.12. Oil pressure should be monitored all the time on the rolling road.

The first start-up for an engine with a newly installed system can be a nightmare. Things will go a lot easier if you take the time to make a few basic checks before you try to start the engine. Remove the spark plugs and isolate the engine's speed signal, so that the ECU doesn't know the engine is turning. Crank the engine and check for oil pressure. With a newly built engine you should keep cranking until oil pressure registers. The last thing you want is to start your new engine and run it at any speed if the oil system isn't working as it should be – it happens.

Next, check the fuel-line pressure. The fuel pump should start and run for a few seconds when you first switch on. If the pump doesn't run, you will be cranking all day and never get so much as a cough from the engine. Ideally, you should have a high-pressure gauge connected to the fuel line. The base pressure will need setting if the regulator is of the adjustable type. The pressure gauge will also tell you if the regulator is plumbed in the right way around. It isn't uncommon to find yourself with 8 or 9 bar base fuel-line pressure because the regulator is pressed shut by the fuel flow being applied in the wrong direction! After having refitted all the plugs and reconnected the speed sensor, you next need to connect your PC and start talking to the ECU.

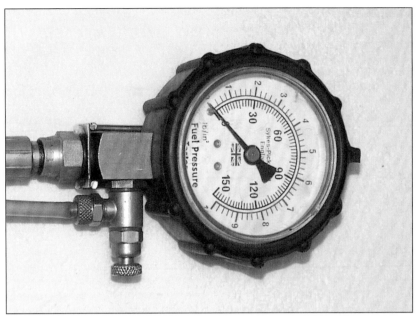

Fig. 12.13. Ideally, you should have a high-pressure fuel gauge connected to the fuel line.

In live communications mode the first check is the air and coolant temperature values. If these are not reading sensible numbers, you are in trouble straight away. The ECU needs to know that the engine is cold before it will add the extra fuel for starting. With a cold engine, the air and coolant temperature readings will be close to each other. If they aren't, you need to check the sensors and wiring.

Next, check the throttle pot operation. If the system uses alignment software, this is the time to carry out the pot alignment. If the system calls for a minimum throttle pot number, make sure that you have it. Some systems start with a high base number and in the event of pot failure the number drops below the minimum, at which point full fuelling is applied.

Fig. 12.14. This live mapping screen is the control centre of the M3DK mapping system.

This is a built-in safety measure, but it can often be more trouble than it's worth. If the pot fails and you only get idle fuelling, the engine isn't going to run on anything but idle anyway. As soon as you open the throttle, the engine will cut, which is equally as safe as running on full fuelling, but you don't flood the engine in the process of finding the fault.

Crank the engine. You should hear the fuel pump re-start, and you should see rpm displayed on the computer screen. The tachometer in the car may not actually read, but you will certainly see the needle flicker as the engine cranks over. All these indicators tell you that the ECU is seeing the engine turning over.

If the engine starts and runs perfectly, then all that's left to do is drive off into the sunset – but it isn't going to happen!

If you are cranking the engine and it doesn't start, how do you know if this is due to fuel or sparks? You may have a spark, but it might be occurring at the wrong time or in the wrong place (wrong cylinder). One very useful piece of diagnostic kit comes in a little spray can – it's called 'Easystart'. A company called 'Bradex' market a spray can of very volatile fuel, which can be used to start reluctant petrol or diesel engines. I use it as a diagnostic aid.

All I do is crank the engine and spray in some Easystart. If the engine fires and runs for a couple of seconds, then I can eliminate the sparks and look at the fuelling. If it just coughs and fires back, then I know the spark, timing or position, is wrong.

You can use this spray on carburettor engines too. If one cylinder isn't firing, a quick spray down the carb intake will either bring that cylinder to life, or it won't. If the cylinder fires, then you have a carb problem. If it doesn't, then you have a spark problem. For the few pounds that it costs Bradex Easystart is a good investment.

If the engine coughs and spits,

Fig. 12.15. 'Easystart' can be used as a useful diagnostic aid.

but will not run, try adding more fuel. You can do this with some systems by trimming the fuel as you crank the engine. With others you need to alter the base map settings and try again.

If the system is running from a distributor trigger, you may have to swing the distributor about to get the engine to start. Once the engine fires and starts to run, use the fuel trim controls to make it run cleanly. Don't worry about cold-start mapping at this stage, just run the engine to warm it up, and check for oil and coolant leaks as you do so. Adjust the idle speed to about 1200rpm to avoid stalling, and then move the idle fuelling until you get a stable idle, or as stable as it's

going to get given the engine spec, big cams, etc.

If the system is triggered from a distributor pick-up, once the engine is running, you must align the distributor. With most systems this means looking at the screen display and confirming the timing using a timing light on the crankshaft pulley. If you have the facility, switch off the interpolation, otherwise the number on the screen may not be the timing figure actually in use. The Emerald system gives you the ability to lock the timing to a fixed reference in degrees. This means that no matter what the speed or load, you get that reference timing, which makes alignment using a timing light a lot

Fig. 12.16. To align the crank pick-up, or distributor, write a map with the same timing all around the idle speed point.

	0	500	1,000	1,500	2,000
0	20	20	20	20	20
1	20	20	20	20	20
2	5	5	2	8	20

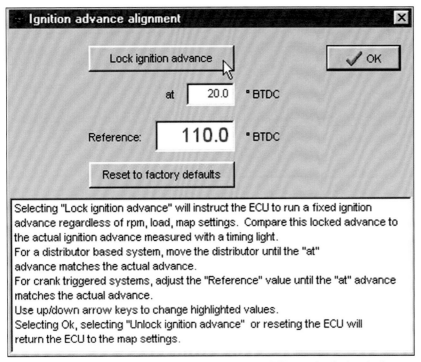

Fig. 12.17. The Emerald system gives you the ability to lock the timing to a fixed reference in degrees, so that no matter what the speed or load, you get that reference timing.

easier. If you have none of these options available, then you must put the same number in the map all around the checking rpm point.

With crankshaft multi-tooth-triggered systems, you should still check the alignment of the pick-up sensor. If this is a factory-fitted trigger, it's unlikely to be out, but home-made triggers are almost certain to need some adjustment. Some systems require that you physically move the pick-up sensor relative to the timing wheel, better ones give you the facility to 'offset' the timing reference in the software. Read the instruction manual that came with the system!

With a full-race, maximum power, engine you will find that a lot of ignition advance on idle helps to stabilise the idle speed. If the engine is anything less than full-race, then a lot of ignition advance on idle is a mistake. If you have a lot of advance, the throttles will have to be closed right down to keep the idle speed low. This means very little air entering the engine, and this in turn makes it very difficult to

get the fuelling right. The resolution of the injectors will not normally be fine enough to enable you to tune into such small volumes of air. Also, on initial throttle opening, the change in airflow is dramatic as a percentage of idle airflow. This makes it very difficult to map for clean progression as you come off idle.

The trick is to run about 8 to 10° of advance at the idle-speed site, but to ramp up the timing below it. At 1000rpm you might have 10° of advance, but at the 500rpm site you put in 35°. If the idle speed starts to falter, then the speed drops and the ignition advances, taking the engine speed up again. The result is a much stronger and more stable idle than is possible with anything other than a mapped ignition system.

The software supplied with this book allows you to set a target rpm and then define the limits of ignition swing. This means that you can put zero in the map at the idle point and let the software get on with it – a much better system!

With full-race engines, the cams are so ineffective at idle that you need a lot of throttle opening just to get an idle, and the problems mentioned previously never come into the picture.

Note that with idle fuelling you may well need a much larger fuel number below the idle site. This is because the air speed drops dramatically from 1000rpm to 500rpm, and most of the idle fuelling will drop out of the air-stream, causing the mixture to go very weak which in turn will cause the engine to stall.

At an early stage of playing with fuel and ignition settings on idle, you need to check the balance of the throttle bodies. A hunting, or rocking, on idle is almost certain to be an out-of-balance problem once the mixture has been sorted. The linkages used on throttle bodies are pretty much a copy of the successful systems used on carburettors. If you are familiar with carburettor balancing, then throttle bodies are no different.

You can buy airflow gauges to push into the bell-mouths, or you can use a length of rubber hose and simply listen to the intake hiss on idle. On a four-cylinder engine with paired throttle bodies, one pair of bodies will be the master set and should contain the idle-speed screw. You adjust the second pair of bodies to this one. On some bodies you have an idle-air bypass screw with a locking nut. You can use these bypass screws to balance the intakes on individual throttles. Note that you should not use this facility to correct the balance where a spindle is twisted. Sometimes a poor throttle return-spring set-up can twist the spindle if the operating arm is on one end and the return spring is on the other. Once you are happy with the balance of the throttle bodies, you should re-align the throttle potentiometer, and finalise idle mixture and ignition timing.

If you get spitting-back in the intake system, this is a sign that the mixture is too weak. The weaker

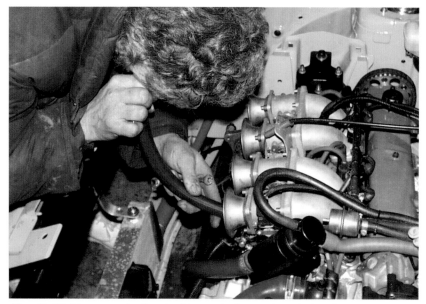

Fig. 12.18. Listen to the intake hiss to balance throttle bodies – or pay big money for a carb balancer.

Fig. 12.19. The air by-pass screws (arrowed) on throttle bodies should not be used to balance out a twisted spindle.

Fig. 12.20. Two-valve engines always run more ignition advance than four-valve engines due to the less efficient combustion chamber design.

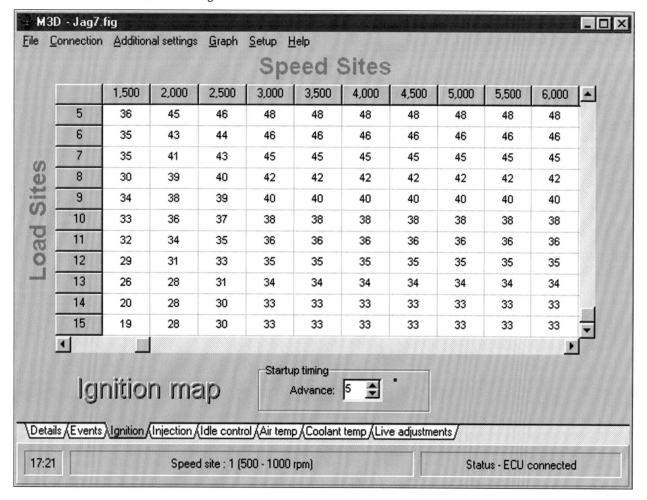

M3D - Jag7.fig												
File _Connection_ _Additional settings_ _Graph_ _Setup_ _Help_												
Speed Sites												
		1,500	2,000	2,500	3,000	3,500	4,000	4,500	5,000	5,500	6,000	
	5	36	45	46	48	48	48	48	48	48	48	
	6	35	43	44	46	46	46	46	46	46	46	
	7	35	41	43	45	45	45	45	45	45	45	
	8	30	39	40	42	42	42	42	42	42	42	
	9	34	38	39	40	40	40	40	40	40	40	
	10	33	36	37	38	38	38	38	38	38	38	
	11	32	34	35	36	36	36	36	36	36	36	
	12	29	31	33	35	35	35	35	35	35	35	
	13	26	28	31	34	34	34	34	34	34	34	
	14	20	28	30	33	33	33	33	33	33	33	
	15	19	28	30	33	33	33	33	33	33	33	

Load Sites

Ignition map

Startup timing
Advance: 5

Details / Events / Ignition / Injection / Idle control / Air temp / Coolant temp / Live adjustments /

17:21	Speed site : 1 (500 - 1000 rpm)	Status - ECU connected

mixture burns so slowly that it is still combusting inside the chamber when the inlet valve opens. The flame then sets light to the incoming fuel in the manifold, and the characteristic spit-back occurs. If you are not using a gas analyser, simply set the mixture to give the smoothest idle without any spitting back in the intake.

Mapping main parameters

With any mapping job, I start by getting the main fuelling and ignition maps right before I worry about cold starts or acceleration fuelling. Having sorted out the idle mixture and ignition timing, I take a look at the ignition map first. If you know the engine, you can write a

map in minutes that will get you 90% of the way there.

The first consideration is maximum advance. As a rough guide, there aren't many two-valve engines that will produce maximum power on less than 27° full advance. I put in a ramp on full-throttle ignition, starting with 18° up to 2000rpm, and making 27° by 3500rpm. On light throttle, I put in 45°, ramping towards full throttle. The starting map for a two-valve engine looks like that shown in Fig. 12.20. For a four-valve-per-cylinder engine, I use 24° as a maximum, and the start-up ignition map looks like that shown in Fig. 12.21.

These are the sort of numbers I use for an unknown engine. If you know that you need 34° maximum advance, then put this number in

the map for full throttle, and adjust the rest of the map accordingly.

If you use these numbers, you *must* check for pinking. If you do not heed this advice, and you end up damaging your engine, don't say that you weren't warned. I can't be there with you, listening for pinking. It's your responsibility to listen out for it. If in doubt – retard. Just as many people wrongly believe that a rich mixture is 'safe', many think that retarded ignition timing can't do any harm. Wrong! If you run too far retarded, the bulk of the heat from combustion goes out of the exhaust. The exhaust will glow red-hot, and so will the exhaust valves. When the head falls off an exhaust valve, you can blame the valve manufacturer, but we will both know who was really at fault!

Fig. 12.21. Note the lower maximum readings of the four-valve engine at full throttle openings.

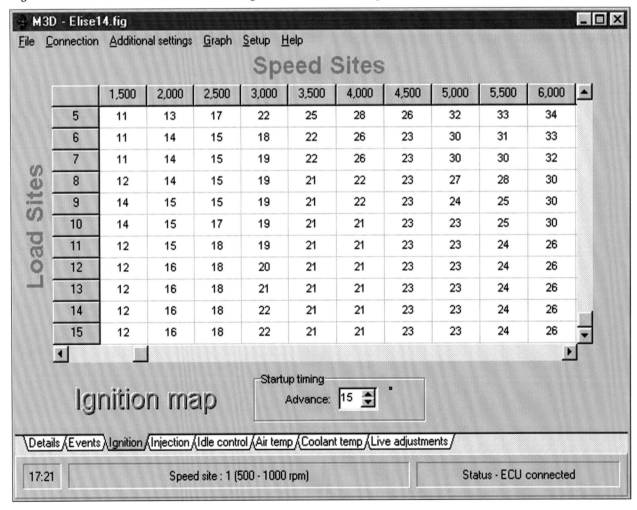

Speed Sites										
	1,500	2,000	2,500	3,000	3,500	4,000	4,500	5,000	5,500	6,000
5	11	13	17	22	25	28	26	32	33	34
6	11	14	15	18	22	26	23	30	31	33
7	11	14	15	19	22	26	23	30	30	32
8	12	14	15	19	21	22	23	27	28	30
9	14	15	15	19	21	22	23	24	25	30
10	14	15	17	19	21	21	23	23	25	30
11	12	15	18	19	21	21	23	23	24	26
12	12	16	18	20	21	21	23	23	24	26
13	12	16	18	21	21	21	23	23	24	26
14	12	16	18	22	21	21	23	23	24	26
15	12	16	18	22	21	21	23	23	24	26

M3D - Elise14.fig

File Connection Additional settings Graph Setup Help

Load Sites

Ignition map

Startup timing
Advance: 15

Details / Events / Ignition / Injection / Idle control / Air temp / Coolant temp / Live adjustments

17:21   Speed site : 1 (500 - 1000 rpm)   Status - ECU connected

Having set up a base map, I sit with the engine running on a stable idle, and simply attempt to 'blip' the throttle. Watch the speed and load sites move on the mapping screen, and feel for what the engine is doing. Most likely you will have big flat spots. You can confirm this on the lambda reader, but you won't have to, as the engine will cough and almost cut dead. The obvious place to start richer is on the load sites below idle, and the speed sites just higher than (to the right of) idle. On our example maps from the Emerald M3DK system, the load reads from top to bottom, and the speed from

left to right. On systems like those from GEMS and Lumenition (UK-based systems), you are moving above and to the right of idle, since the map starts with idle at the bottom and moves up with increasing load. DTA systems, again UK-based, have speed reading from top to bottom, and load from left to right. There is no industry standard.

Once I have an engine capable of moving off idle without stalling, I drive to 2500rpm and start my mapping. Get into the habit straight away of checking the coolant temperature. This should be displayed on the mapping

screen, although some systems infuriatingly hide it away and rely on a flashing warning code. I want to know when I am *heading* for trouble, not when I have *arrived*!

On light throttle, adjust the fuelling until the engine runs cleanly, and work down the first few load sites, perhaps to one-third throttle. The software supplied with this book has a 'target' with a moving cross. When you get the cross dead-centre on the target, you are right in the middle of the speed and load site. The throttle moves the cross down with increased load, and the rpm moves it left to right – in the same way as the maps. Stop the engine and take a look at the map. Remember that no matter how careful you were in aligning the map site, the system will be interpolating slightly in two directions. If you had to put in a number much bigger than those to the left or right, the final number when you have completed mapping will be smaller, because you will then have put the right settings into the adjacent boxes. Check the graph shown in Fig. 12.22 for a clearer understanding. Next, I put some numbers into the map on either side of the mapped points. Using the map shown in Fig. 12.23 as an example, you will see that these numbers are all over the place. This map should be more like the one shown in Fig. 12.24. Now I can go back and look at the same points again. At this stage, it's worth considering the end use of the engine. If it's a racer, and I'm mapping at an engine rpm site that is off cam, I don't worry too much about fuel consumption, the engine just has to run cleanly in order to reach the operating range. For a road engine, you need a much weaker mixture at certain points in the map, often coinciding with certain speed limits. In the UK, I map at 70mph (legal limit) in top gear for best fuel economy.

Don't aim for a lambda of one, or a stoichiometric mixture, other than at idle, and only then if the engine likes to run this way, or

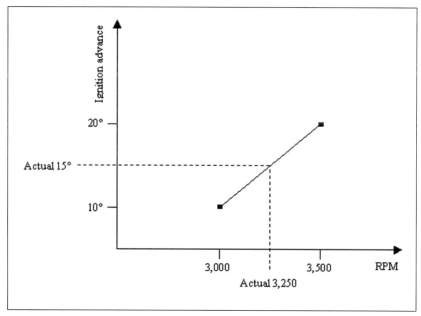

Fig. 12.22. Interpolation draws a straight line between points – there isn't a 'step' as such between sites.

Fig. 12.23. Way-out numbers will mean that interpolation makes life very difficult.

500	1,000	1,500
49	23	37
75	56	63
90	70	80
95	75	90
100	80	95

Fig. 12.24. The answer is to fill in the area with sensible guesstimates so that the interpolation has a minimal effect.

500	1,000	1,500
39	33	27
67	66	53
82	80	70
86	85	80
92	90	85

needs to. Where a catalytic converter is fitted, you should run with closed-loop mode switched off (disabled). On light throttle, you can safely run weak mixtures, even down to the point of misfire, without doing any damage. There simply isn't the volume of fuel going through the engine to generate enough heat to melt anything, or to heat the combustion chamber to the point of detonation. It's only as you begin to open the throttle that you get into the danger area.

With a lambda mixture reader you can squeeze the throttle to the higher load sites and take an instant mixture reading. A quick on/off with the throttle pedal enables you to get a feel for what is happening to the mixture. If the mixture reader instantly goes weak, then trim in more fuel and take another look. If the mixture goes rich, trim fuel out. Once the lambda reader shows that the mixture is somewhere in the ball-park, save the fuelling number and stop the engine. Now take another look at the map.

As with initial fuelling, you want to look at the sites around your target area. Fill in the adjacent sites with similar values, and re-check under load. Now is the time to turn your attention to the power output readout. Get back to the target load site under power, and double check the lambda reader. If it's still in the ball-park, check the power output and trim in more fuel. What you want is the fuel number that gives the maximum power output. In practice you will find that you have a fairly wide tolerance for maximum power. Between half and three-quarters throttle, I aim for the least amount of fuel that makes maximum power. From three-quarters to full throttle I always leave a little excess fuel in the map, not enough to reduce power, but enough to give me peace of mind that the mixture isn't too weak. Call me a chicken!

As I map with the Emerald system, I count the number of keyboard taps so that I can always return to the starting point. With this system there is a 'trim clear' key so I can add or subtract fuel and then press **'Clear'** as I watch the power output. If I seem to have a made a gain from trimming, this will disappear as I clear the trim, confirming my adjustment. Once I am happy with the new value, I put it back via the trim button and save the load site setting by pressing the **'Enter'** key.

An alternative is to use the 'trim box' or what most people calls 'wheels'. Using the software supplied with this book, you simply add trim to the fuel and ignition, or take it away, and press the green button to store. This cancels the dialled-in trim, puts the new site into the map, and kills the trim-box function. You then zero the dials, press the green button again, and the wheels are functioning once more. Personally I like the keyboard, but that may be only because I am used to it. A lot of professional operators prefer the wheels system.

Having mapped the first column, I then move on to the next load site and repeat the process down to full throttle. I find it important to keep looking at the overall picture in the initial mapping stages, putting in 'sensible' values either side of my target sites. Once I have mapped all the load sites down to full throttle at 2500rpm, I take a good look at the map. At this stage you can put in some approximate numbers, so that when you approach an unmapped site it will at least run the engine, rather than misfiring or cutting out altogether. Below 2500rpm I increase fuel numbers in even steps, and above 2500rpm I put the same number into each site.

All engines vary, and depending on the manifold design you will get varying degrees of fuel drop-out with different engine rpm. However, you almost always get some drop-out as the revs decrease, which means that increasing fuel numbers are required with lower rpm. With increasing revs, you often find that you need smaller fuel numbers on light throttle because more of the fuel is carried into the combustion chamber (higher air speed means less drop-out). But, with higher rpm and more throttle, the numbers frequently go up, depending on the breathing characteristics of the engine (dictated by the camshaft, exhaust and inlet tract lengths, etc).

Having mapped the idle and initial throttle opening by ear, and the one speed site down to full throttle, I always map the lower rpm range next. I never spend a lot of time trying to get full throttle at low rpm. No driver should be expecting a competition engine to pull full throttle at 2000rpm or below. If you decide to map all the way to full throttle on an engine with big camshafts and throttle bodies, don't be too surprised to see the fuel numbers *decreasing* on the last few load sites towards full throttle, and the engine making *less* power on full throttle than part throttle. With the butterflies wide open, the reverse flow is higher than with them only part open – at low rpm you don't have the air speed to overcome the natural reverse flow of a wide-overlap camshaft. Personally, at these low revs I just put in a number that I know will be too rich, to prevent the engine from stalling if the driver finds the wrong gear at the wrong time.

Having mapped/guessed the low rpm load sites, I next look at going above 2500rpm. There are two ways of going about this. You can move along the rpm sites, mapping from light to full throttle as you go, or you can select the load site and increase the revs, moving along the rpm sites, but staying on the same load position. If the engine is new, or freshly built, I prefer to map the light-throttle sites first to get some miles on the engine. At 3000rpm I open the throttle to the first load site and adjust the fuelling, saving the site number once I am happy with it. Then I hold the load at this position, and increase the revs by backing off the dyno load, moving up the rpm range to the next site (same throttle opening). I then map that site and move on again.

Before long, you reach the point where the revs no longer increase as you back off the dyno. At this stage you simply don't have enough throttle to drive the car above that point. For example, no engine is going to get to 60mph on an almost closed throttle (for example load site one). Once you reach this point, simply fill in the same numbers to the end of the rpm range, and take the engine back to the starting point – in this case it was 3000rpm. Open the throttle some more, and keep repeating the process down to about half throttle. By then any new engine will either be loosened up or broken!

Now you can map the heavy load sites, and this is where you have to work a little quicker. Power tends to fade as the combustion chamber heats up – a static engine isn't running in its natural state. Normally engines accelerate under heavy load, but we are holding station with the aid of the dyno load cell. If you hold for too long while you look for the optimum setting, the engine will start to lose power and you will start to get confused. Set the engine rpm back to 3000, and apply the load to the required site. Check the lambda sensor reading, and back off if it isn't on the rich side. It's better to run rich and come back down to the optimum setting, rather than the other way around. Once you know that you are somewhere close, put the load back on and watch the power output as you reduce the fuelling. Power will probably climb initially and then stay the same for several taps of the adjusting key. You will find that you have a range of mixtures where power remains the same. For these sites I try to get into the middle of this adjustment range.

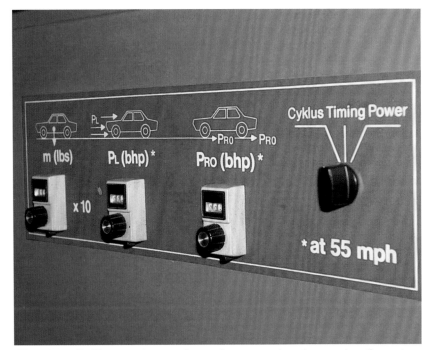

Fig. 12.25. Rolling road controls can be set to alter the acceleration rate, which in turn affects the results. An excellent way of fiddling the final power!

For example, if I have maximum power from a fuel number of 125 up to 132, then I set the map to 129. Running a touch rich helps to reduce the chance of detonation, but don't overdo it. A lot of people are simply scared of weak mixtures and they over-fuel to the point of black-smoking.

As with the lighter load sites, once you have established one full-throttle setting, take a look at the map and put similar numbers around this point. By now you will have built up something of a picture of how the final map will look. With the higher rpm full-load sites I never hold the power full-on and then make adjustments, it's too hard on the engine. I check them by doing acceleration power runs.

Set the dyno to 'timing' and take a full power curve. On my rolling road this means driving very gently up to fourth gear and then flooring the throttle. Watch the lambda sensor like a hawk as the revs rise, and if the engine looks like running weak, lift off and note the rpm site. Modify the fuel number and try again. If you mapped on steady state up to 5000rpm, then using the same fuel number up to peak revs at 8000rpm plus is normally safe. The maximum fuel number is at peak torque, and after that, usually, it drops away a little – but not always. Remember that the fuel number is the injector duration, nothing else. If some of the fuel is lost out of the exhaust due to valve overlap, or an unfavourable exhaust length, then sometimes you need a larger fuel number to produce less torque. Always give the engine what it wants, not what you think it should have.

Having recorded a power curve, check where peak torque is, and how high you need to rev before the power drops away. Try a second run with a small amount of additional fuel. I simply trim in some extra fuel and run the engine up trimmed, rather than re-writing the map. Check to see if the power improves. If not, try reducing the fuel a little, again using the trim, and compare the results. By plotting torque curves over each other you can build up a picture of what the engine wants to see in

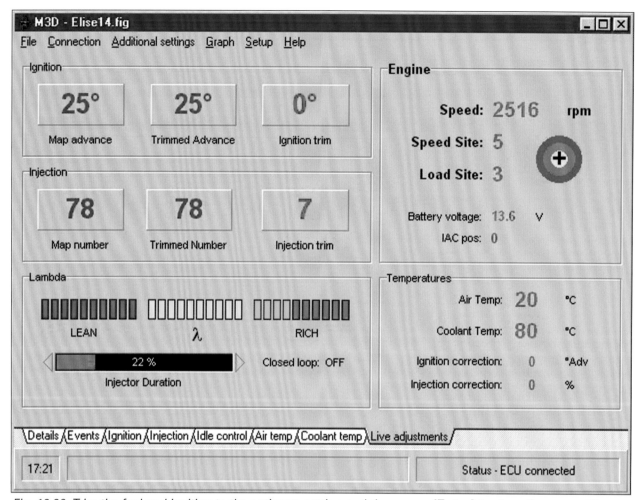

Fig. 12.26. Trim the fuel and ignition to the optimum setting and then press **'Enter'** *to store the new settings in the map.*

terms of fuel numbers. Having established a working fuel map turn to the ignition.

Mapping the ignition on light loads is exactly the same deal as mapping the fuel numbers except it's a lot easier. Just look out for optimum power at the wheels and run *as little advance as you need to*. Just because the engine will stand more advance without pinking, there is no reason to run with it. Always aim for the minimum best timing (MBT).

You can check the flat-out high rpm ignition timing with acceleration power runs, just as described previously for fuelling. Take a power curve, then use the trim to retard the timing by 2°. Carry out another power run, and compare the results. Once you

have the optimum overall power curve for ignition, look at the torque curve. You can almost always run more advance at higher rpm as the torque drops away. Get into the map and try adding more advance where the torque drops off. Take another power curve and check again. Keep juggling the advance until you get no gain. Quite often you see timing of 28/30° at peak torque (usually around 5000rpm), but as much as 36/38° at 8000rpm or more. These figures are for a two-valves-per-cylinder engine; four-valve engines tend to run higher rpm, but the principle still holds true, even if the maximum numbers are lower.

Provided the engine doesn't constantly run too hot and I don't have to wait for it to cool down, I

reasonably expect to get a close working base map within three hours, start to finish. After that you can spend another ten hours refining the map, but you will have already had the lion's share of the available power. If you are very concerned about emissions and fuel consumption, you can spend a lot more time working the map – but if that's the case you are reading the wrong book! For a competition engine, after three hours mapping, you should be close enough to the optimum to go racing.

Cranking enrichment

With big cams and big throttle bodies, the air speed when cranking on start-up is very low.

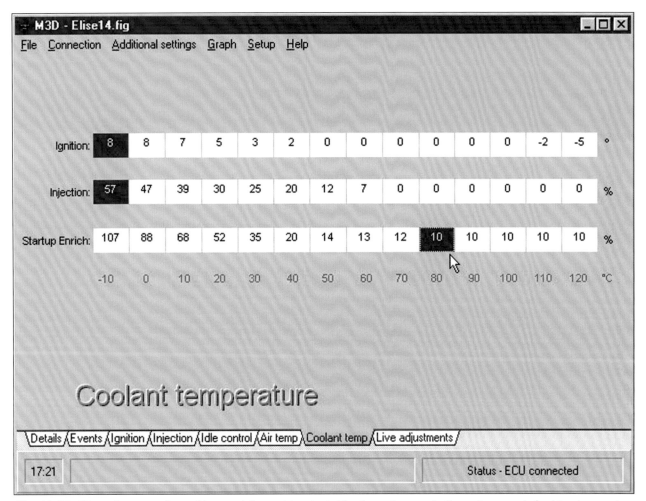

| | -10 | 0 | 10 | 20 | 30 | 40 | 50 | 60 | 70 | 80 | 90 | 100 | 110 | 120 | °C |

Fig. 12.27. All engines need cranking enrichment to start. The low air speed allows too much fuel to drop out otherwise.

For this reason a lot of fuel drops out of the air stream and puddles on the manifold floor. You must have the facility to add extra fuel on cranking, even with a hot engine. Most systems work by adding a lot of extra fuel on initial cranking, with the enrichment decaying away after a few seconds. If the engine doesn't catch within the first five seconds, it is less likely to do so with continued cranking, because the enrichment is decaying away.

Failure to start for hot race engines is sometimes down to the starter motor struggling to overcome high compression, but often it's due simply to bad mapping. I've seen competitors who leave their engine running all day because once they switch off it won't re-start. The cure is almost always more cranking enrichment, but if you don't know this, the cause can become a mystery because once started the engine runs fine. In percentage terms, some engines need as little as 5% enrichment when hot, some need 30%. While you're mapping on the rollers, it's an ideal time to try more, then less cranking enrichment, until the engine hot-starts with regularity.

Cold starting takes a lot more cranking enrichment, and the only way to find out how much is to try starting from cold. With cold settings I tend to go for too rich, rather than too weak, but you have to avoid wetting the plugs. The biggest problem is that you only tend to get one go at cold-start mapping, because as soon as the engine starts it begins to warm up. This isn't a job you can tackle with much success in the summer.

Acceleration fuelling

With snap throttle opening you get a sudden in-rush of air into the engine, and the fuel doesn't have time to exit the injector before the air is long gone. You get a flat-spot, which is a cough before the engine accelerates. On a carburettor you have a mechanical pump which forces fuel out into the air stream, preventing the mixture from going weak and thus eliminating the flat spot.

With fuel injection you have no mechanical means of adding extra fuel. The software has to read the rate of throttle opening, decide that additional fuel is needed, and make the correction. With most systems you have the option of increasing the amount of fuel, and often the time period over which this enrichment takes place. More sophisticated systems allow you to adjust the level of extra fuel, how long you hold that level, and at what rate the extra enrichment decays away.

The time equation may be in seconds, or in injector triggering events. You may also have the option of switching off the acceleration enrichment at a given rpm point. This is because the engine responds much more quickly if it's already running at high speed than it does when accelerating from idle.

Mapping all these parameters takes time, and some engines are a lot more trouble than others. A lightweight four-cylinder engine with an aluminium flywheel and throttle bodies requires a lot less correction than a heavy V8 running on a stock plenum-chamber intake.

The test most people make is to snap the throttle to the floor from idle. In reality this is unrealistic, because you don't floor the pedal out of gear. The real test is to drive the car and snap the throttle open from low rpm. The level of enrichment required depends on the intake design, but also on how well you have mapped the speed and load sites.

Early racing carburettors didn't have any correction for snap throttle opening. You simply set the mixture rich, and when you opened the throttle suddenly the additional air weakened the mixture, but not enough to cause a bad flat spot. If you have mapped the engine rich at low rpm and light load, then you will have little problem with acceleration enrichment. However, you *will* have problems with light-throttle running. Over-rich mapping at light throttle/low rpm means driving around the paddock with the engine hunting and shaking like a jelly on a plate. People will put this down to the 'wild' camshaft, but it's actually a mapping fault.

Personally, as long as the engine drives okay, I don't worry about acceleration fuelling from idle. In fact, I have a suspicion that clever as these electronic systems are, you can't map them to give the same snap throttle response as a carburettor – although I may be wrong.

Cold-start mapping

Once the engine starts okay from cold, you have to wait a few seconds for the cranking enrichment to decay away. What you are then left with is the engine running on warm-up enrichment. This is a correction to the map in relation to coolant temperature.

The system I adopt is to stabilise the engine with the trim key and note the settings, particularly the engine temperature. I then go into the warm-up map and make the changes. If you work quickly, you can check your new settings before the engine moves to the next temperature site. It may take you several goes to get this to your liking, but you need a cold engine

Fig. 12.28. Acceleration enrichment can generally be switched off at higher rpm – you simply don't need it.

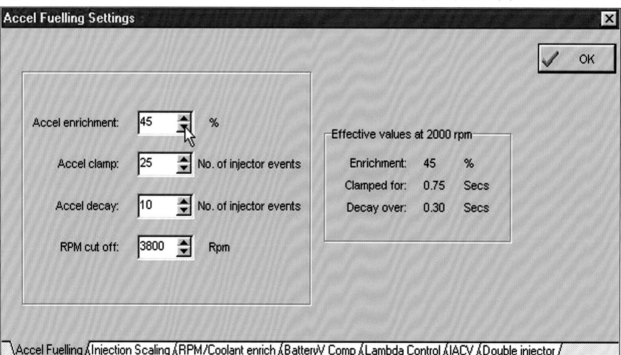

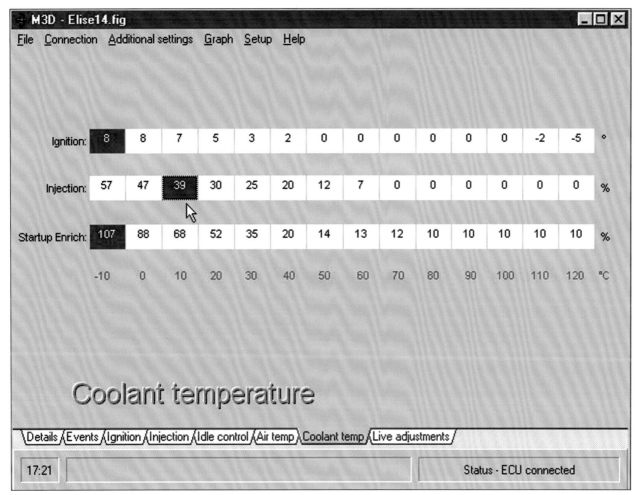

Fig. 12.29. Cold-start settings can only be arrived at by experiment. You generally get just one chance each morning.

to start with. This means waiting, preferably overnight, for the engine to cool down between mapping sessions. Temperature correction for cold running is something you have to tackle over a period of time.

If your system links coolant temperature to ignition timing, you can add some more advance with a cold engine. This helps to increase cold idle rpm, and makes for smoother pick-up with a cold engine. We are talking warm-up phase here, not driving hard with a cold motor. Once the engine reaches 40°C, you can take out any additional advance.

If you must drive while you warm up the engine, be aware that some competition systems are not really suited to this. Some systems only allow for one cold-start site, which then interpolates to the hot-running temperature. Some systems allow mapping at various temperature break points, but make no allowance for engine speed. With the right cold-running mixture at idle, you need less enrichment with increased revs. Quite simply, the higher engine rpm increases the air speed, and less fuel drops out of the air-stream, creating a richer mixture as far as the engine is concerned.

The way around this is to have a coolant temperature correction against engine rpm. This allows you to reduce the coolant temperature correction with increasing revs. For example, you can reduce cold-running correction by 20% at 1500rpm, by 30% at 2500rpm and by 40% at 3500rpm – or whatever it takes to get the engine to rev cleanly when cold. This takes some doing because you have to remember that while you're adjusting the fuel at 20°C, the engine may well have moved on to 30°C. You must keep a watchful eye on the engine temperature display. The plus side is that cold-run mapping isn't frantic, there's no drama or danger of engine damage. If you make a mess of it you can always start again in the morning.

Chapter 13

Using the Emerald M3DK mapping software

Introduction

Engine management mapping software has a reputation for being 'difficult' to use. This myth has resulted from very early DOS-based mapping systems which truly were a nightmare to find your way around – even computer programmers had difficulty in locating the various maps and correction systems, while the average rolling-road operator often gave up in frustration. I've been there myself – you know it's just a question of pressing the right button, but you really can't figure out which button to press. Stabbing in the dark often has unexpected and sometimes unpleasant results!

By now, hopefully you will have found the computer disc supplied with this book, which contains the operating software for the Emerald 32-bit ECU. I have supplied this system simply because I had a major input into its design. I wanted a software system that was both logical and easy to use – easy being a relative term! The system has been developed from experience on the rolling road. For example, the software can read and programme the ECU while the engine is running. This avoids the necessity to stop and re-start the engine to make adjustments – if the engine being mapped has a flat battery, or weak starter motor/starter motor wiring you can lose a lot of time using jump leads or battery boosters. Racing cars often have tiny batteries to save weight, and you are lucky to get two starts out of them, let alone dozens on the trot.

You can jump straight from map to map, and read/programme the ECU from any position in the software. A colour-code system tells you which sites you have mapped live (red), which sites you have

entered as a guessed setting (blue), and which ones you haven't touched (black). You can clear the colours as you go along, or not, as you please. The target symbol on the live-mapping screen allows you to get right in the middle of the map site, and the bar graph, which shows the mixture reading of the lambda sensor, is a real time saver. The second bar graph showing injector duration tells you if you are running out of injector duration, which will mean that you need larger injectors, or a higher base fuel-line pressure. In the event of either of these changes being necessary, you can enter the changes into the software, and the maps will re-calculate so that you can carry on mapping as if nothing had changed – you don't have to start again! The best way to get to know the system is to play with the software, and loading instructions are included for non-computer types like myself.

Installing the M3DK Windows engine mapping software

The M3DK Windows mapping software is written in 32-bit code, which means it can be operated using MS Windows 95 onwards.

The software files are provided in self-extracting form on the CD supplied with this book. The programme cannot be operated from the CD, and will have to be installed on the hard drive of your PC.

To install the programme, insert the CD and proceed as follows:

1   From the Windows **'Start'** menu, select **'Run'**.
2   When asked for a file name, type **x:setup.exe** (where **x** = the identifying letter for your CD drive) and press **'Enter'**.
3   Follow the on-screen instructions to complete

installation. After each stage, click on the **'Next'** button to proceed to the following stage. Note that the default location on your PC's hard drive for the files is **C:\Program Files\Emerald\M3DK Demo** – this can be changed by clicking on the **'Browse'** button and selecting your chosen location.

4   When the installation procedure has been completed, click on the **'Finish'** button to leave the installation programme.

5   To launch the software, from the Windows **'Start'** menu, select **'Programs'**, **'Emerald'**, **'M3DK demo'**. (If you have chosen an alternative location for the **'M3DK demo'** launch icon during the software installation, you will need to select the icon from this alternative location.)

6   When the software is launched an **'Introduction'** window will appear. Once you have read the introduction, click on the **'Done'** button to display the main software windows. When using the software, the **'Introduction'** window can be displayed at any time by selecting it from the **'Help'** menu.

An introduction to the M3DK Windows engine mapping software

This version of the M3DK demonstration software is a special release for this Haynes *Engine Management* book. You will find a 'floating' window over all the screens, which is not mentioned in the following general text. The 'floating' window can be moved by clicking and dragging on the title bar at the top of the window. The function of this window is to allow you to drive the software as if it were connected to an engine. You will have throttle control, plus rpm and temperature inputs, etc. You can use these to input engine data and see the result as if you were mapping a real engine.

For example you can set the engine on light throttle with low rpm as if it were on idle, and alter the fuel and ignition maps. Selecting **'Enter'** will then save these settings into the maps. This will give the newcomer to engine mapping a much better feel for the software and how it works in the real world.

The M3DK Windows mapping software consists of a paged main window. Rather than having separate

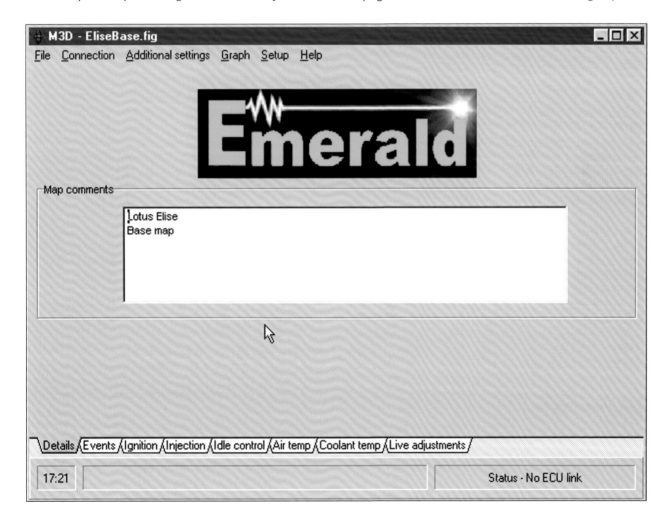

M3D - Elise14.fig

File   Connection   Additional settings   Graph   Setup   Help

Speed Sites

	0	500	1,000	1,500	2,000	2,500	3,000	3,500	4,000	4,500
0	55	39	28	27	26	25	22	20	20	17
1	70	65	61	53	46	41	42	39	37	33
2	88	80	75	70	58	54	51	50	50	47
3	93	85	80	80	67	65	62	61	60	58
4	98	90	85	85	75	73	75	71	67	65
5	98	90	85	85	77	78	78	79	81	75
6	98	90	85	87	79	83	86	88	90	85
7	100	92	87	89	79	84	90	93	96	90
8	100	92	87	87	78	82	92	92	100	99
9	100	92	87	85	78	82	92	92	100	101
10	100	92	87	85	78	82	92	92	101	101
11	100	92	87	85	79	82	92	95	101	101
12	100	92	87	85	79	82	92	95	102	102

Load Sites

Injection map

\Details /Events /Ignition /Injection /Idle control /Air temp /Coolant temp /Live adjustments /

windows for different parts of the map settings, most of the settings are accessible through separate pages within the main window.

For example, page 1 is the **'Details'** page that contains user mapping notes which are stored along with the maps, page 4 is the **'Injection map'** page and contains the 16 x 32 site injection map.

The different functions of the 'map' are grouped into these separate pages to make the information easier to digest.

The M3DK main screen also displays other useful information. Along the top of the screen is the 'Title bar' that shows the name of the current map that is held in memory. 'M3DK' followed by the map name indicates that the map is a file that has been loaded from disk. 'ECU' followed by the map name indicates that the current map has been read from the ECU itself. Whenever a map is saved to disk, the 'Title bar' will indicate that the map is now a filed map.

At the very bottom of the main screen is a 3-section 'Status bar'. The first section is a clock which will display the same setting as your PC clock. The second section is for general information, and may display additional help or information depending on the task in hand.

The third section of the status bar shows the ECU communications status. With no communications link to the ECU (no power to ECU or comms lead not connected), the status will display **'Status – No ECU link'**. As soon as the M3DK control software receives valid data the status will display **'Status – ECU connected'**. If a communications link is lost at any time (ie, by disconnecting comms lead or disconnecting the power to the ECU) the status will revert to **'Status – No ECU link'**, but will now be coloured red to indicate a possible problem.

Navigating your way around the software

As with most Windows software, the mouse pointer is the primary input device but this is not always convenient, especially when operating from a laptop computer. If it is either impractical or just too slow to use the mouse pointer, the keyboard can be used instead. The M3DK software can be operated entirely from the keyboard using key shortcuts for many functions.

To navigate around the various settings within a page, using a keyboard, repeatedly press the **'Tab'** key until the cursor moves to the required setting. If there is only one possible map setting within any particular page or screen, this input is active automatically.

Selecting with the mouse pointer or cursor activates a particular map setting. Various methods are used to change the value of an activated map setting. These methods will depend on the type of setting you are trying to change.

The map pages

The pages available are shown as 'Tabs' near the bottom of the main screen. **Note**: *Other software versions may have different tabs to those shown in the example below*. To move to another page simply click the desired tab with the mouse pointer. As an alternative to using the mouse, you can use the shortcut keys as follows:

'F1'...Details screen.

'F2'...Events screen (various rpm & temperature activated events).

'F3'...Ignition map.

'F4'...Injection map.

'F5'...Idle control settings.

'F6'...Air temperature correction settings.

'F7'...Coolant temperature correction settings.

'F8'...Live adjustments.

Each screen contains various data settings that can be changed using the mouse and/or keyboard. The mouse is not specifically required; any task can be accomplished from the keyboard.

'TAB'...Moves the cursor to the next available data entry control on screen (pressing **'TAB'** repeatedly, will cycle the cursor around all the controls).

Details / Events / Ignition / Injection / Idle control / Air temp / Coolant temp / Live adjustments /

The Menu

Pressing the **'ALT'** key activates the menu. Pressing the **'ALT'** key again returns the cursor control to the main M3DK window. Once the menu is active, you can navigate around the various functions using the cursor keys. Move the highlight until it is on the desired function and press **'Enter'** to select it. Navigating using the mouse is just a case of clicking on the desired menu heading and then on the desired function in the drop-down menu.

Menu headings

'File'
'Open map file'
'Save map file'
'Exit'

'Connection'
'Read ECU'
'Program ECU'

'Additional settings'
'Accel Fuelling'
'Injection Scaling'
'RPM Correction for Coolant Enrichment'
'Battery Voltage Compensation'
'Lambda Control'
'Idle Air Control'
'Double Injector Control'

'Graph'
'Plot Graph'

'Setup'
'Throttle Pot'
'Distributer / Pickup'
'Immobiliser'
'ECU Configuration'

'Help'
'Introduction'
'Diag data'

Using the software

The eight pages of the main M3DK window contain the bulk of the map settings; additional settings and functions are also available through the menu at the top of the screen.

'Details' (F1)

When first loaded, the M3DK software will default to

this page. Details or comments that are attached to the map currently loaded into memory will be shown in the **'Map comments'** text box.

The map comments text box can hold up to 255 characters. Once the limit is reached you will not be able to enter any more text. Note that 'spaces' after any text also count as characters. If you find that you are not able to enter as much information as you would like, check that there are no spaces following your text.

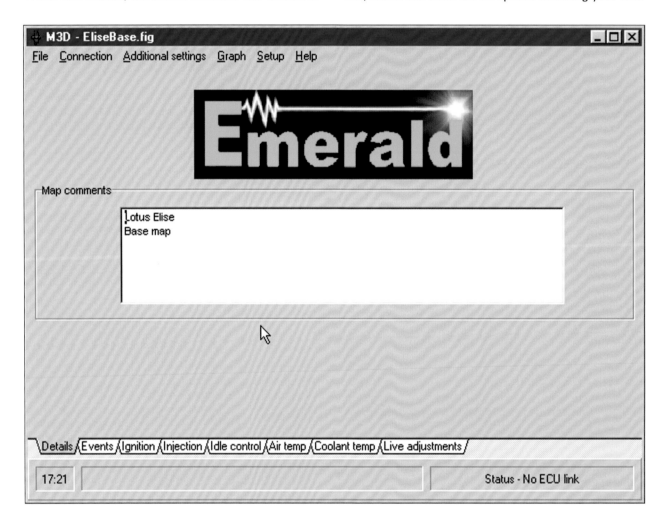

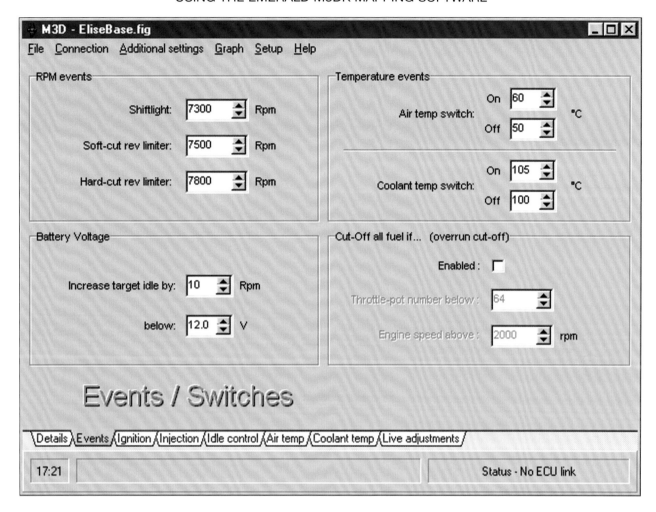

'Events' (F2)

This page contains a number of settings that dictate the ECU's response to certain input conditions. These settings are laid out in four areas, **'RPM events'**, **'Battery Voltage'**, **'Temperature events' and 'Cut-Off all fuel if . . .'**.

'RPM events'
To change one of the **'RPM events'** settings, highlight the setting you want to change and increase or decrease the rpm number by pressing the up/down

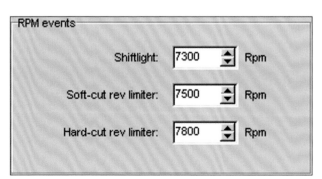

arrow keys. With each key press, the number will change in 50rpm steps; holding the arrow key down will rapidly change the value. To change these values with the mouse pointer, simply click on the appropriate up/down arrow button beside the value you want to change.

When the engine rpm has reached the **'Shiftlight'** rpm, the ECU shiftlight output will switch to earth and, if fitted, will illuminate a dashboard-mounted warning lamp. Normally this is used to indicate a maximum safe rpm, or a desired change-up point.

Once the **'Soft-cut rev limiter'** rpm has been reached, and depending on the ECU software version, either every third ignition spark (4-cylinder system) will be cut or the ignition will be retarded to zero degrees advance. Cutting the ignition sparks in this way ensures that each cylinder is cut in turn, giving a 'smooth' rev limit. Later ECU versions retard the ignition to get the same 'smooth' effect, but you will still hear what sounds like a misfire as the engine power is reduced and then increased again as the rpm falls below the soft-cut rpm threshold. Although this type of rev-limiter does *reduce* engine power, it is still possible for the engine to continue accelerating and over-rev.

When the **'Hard-cut rev limiter'** rpm is reached, all ignition sparks and fuel pulses will stop until the engine rpm falls below this rpm setting. It is possible for the engine to exceed this rpm setting by mechanically over-revving, even though the engine is effectively switched off, ie when down-changing into too low a gear.

'Temperature events'

The ECU has two general-purpose switched outputs that can be activated by the air and coolant temperatures as measured by the ECU. These outputs switch to earth when active. The coolant switch output can be used to control an electric cooling-fan

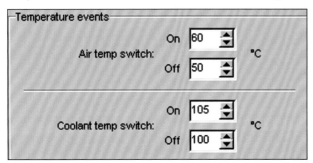

relay. Having a separate **'On'** and **'Off'** setting means you can set the temperature at which the cooling fan switches on and also the temperature the engine must cool down to before switching the fan off.

The air-temperature switch will not be used in most cases, and only certain ECU versions will have this function enabled. This function can have various uses, eg for switching on a charge cooler when the inlet-air temperature reaches a given threshold.

To adjust these on/off values press **'Tab'** to activate to desired setting, and then use the up/down arrow keys to change the setting.

'Ignition' (F3)

The ignition map is a 16 load-site x 32 speed-site 'look-up table'. Each cell contains a number that is an ignition timing setting in degrees BTDC (before top dead centre).

The speed sites are spaced left to right every 500rpm, starting at site 0 (0 to 500rpm).

The load sites, rows 0 to 15 (0 is closed throttle, 15 is full throttle) are spaced so as to bias the sites towards closed throttle where there is the greatest percentage change in air flow for a given degree of throttle movement. In the example

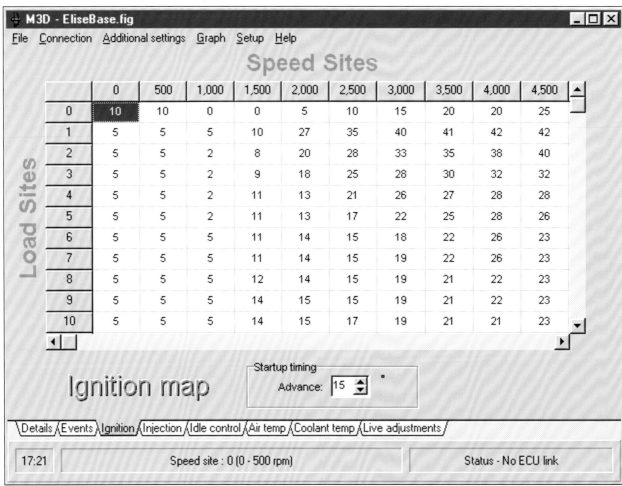

above, only 10 of the 15 sites are visible due to screen size.

As rpm and throttle position change, the ECU looks at the cell for the relevant speed/load conditions to determine the ignition timing. If the current engine speed or load condition falls between the sites in the map, then the value is interpolated between the nearest sites, ie the two nearest speed sites and two nearest load sites. By calculating an interpolated setting, there is no step in value as a load or speed condition crosses a site boundary.

The start-up timing is a separate value from the main map. While cranking, the main map is ignored and the timing is determined by the start-up timing value (regardless of load). When the engine speed has risen above 500rpm, the software switches to the ignition map to determine ignition timing; the software will **not** use the start-up timing value again unless the engine has completely stalled or the ECU is reset.

The values in the ignition map can be changed in various ways. Use the cursor arrow keys to move the blue highlight to the desired speed/load site cell. Press 'Enter' to bring up the **'Insert IGNITION map data'** window as shown below.

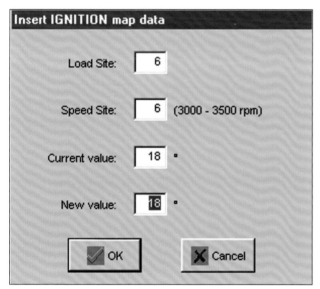

You are reminded of the speed/load site of the cell you have selected and also the current ignition advance value. If you want to change the ignition advance, type in the new value and press **'Enter'** (or select **'OK'**). Pressing the **'Escape'** key or selecting **'Cancel'** will return you to the map unchanged. Allowable values are 0°BTDC to 60°BTDC; negative or fractional values will not be accepted.

An alternative way to change individual map values is to use the **'+'** and **'–'** keys. These will increase/decrease the value in the currently highlighted map cell by 1°.

By blocking a map area (using the drag-mouse method or by pressing and holding the **'Shift'** key while moving the cursor with the arrow keys) you are able to change the value of more than one site at a time. With an area of the map highlighted, the **'+'** and **'–'** keys can be used to increase/decrease those values by 1°. Pressing **'Enter'** with an area selected will bring up the **'Block map function'** window.

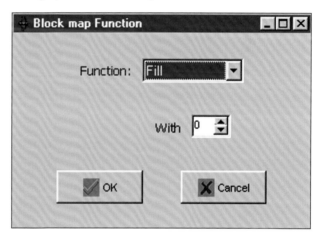

The available functions are **'Fill'**, **'Add'** or **'Subtract'**. Use the up/down arrow keys to select the desired function (or use the mouse). Press **'Tab'** to select the value to fill, add or subtract, then type in the value. Press **'Enter'** to perform the function, or press **'Escape'** to abort.

![M3D - EliseBase.fig application window showing the Injection map. The title 'Speed Sites' is at top with column headers 0, 500, 1,000, 1,500, 2,000, 2,500, 3,000, 3,500, 4,000, 4,500. 'Load Sites' labels the rows 0-10.]

	0	500	1,000	1,500	2,000	2,500	3,000	3,500	4,000	4,500
0	55	39	28	27	26	25	22	20	20	17
1	70	65	61	53	46	41	42	39	37	33
2	88	80	75	70	58	54	51	50	50	47
3	93	85	80	80	67	65	62	61	60	58
4	98	90	85	85	75	73	75	71	67	65
5	98	90	85	85	77	78	78	79	81	75
6	98	90	85	87	79	83	86	88	90	85
7	100	92	87	89	79	84	90	93	96	90
8	100	92	87	87	78	82	92	92	100	99
9	100	92	87	85	78	82	92	92	100	101
10	100	92	87	85	78	82	92	92	101	101

Injection map

\Details /Events /Ignition /Injection /Idle control /Air temp /Coolant temp /Live adjustments /

| 17:21 | Speed site : 0 (0 - 500 rpm) | Status - No ECU link |

'Injection' (F4)

The injection map functions in much the same way as the ignition map. Note that there is no start-up value – the injector pulse-width duration is taken from the main injection map at all times.

The injection map values determine how long the injectors are switched on for. The values can range from 0 to 255 (0 milliseconds to 15.5 milliseconds). As with the ignition map, the final injection value is interpolated between the nearest sites, ie the two nearest speed sites and two nearest load sites.

Use the '+' and '–' keys to increase/decrease the value individual sites or blocked areas. Pressing 'Enter' will bring up the 'Insert INJECTION map data' window as shown below. This window will also display the injection duration (in milliseconds) that this current value represents, and also the percentage of available time this injector will be open for.

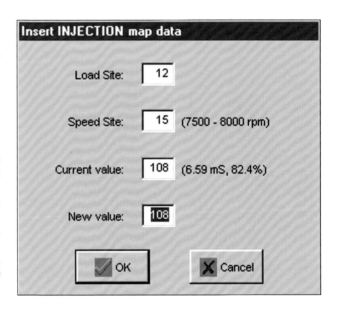

Insert INJECTION map data

Load Site: 12

Speed Site: 15 (7500 - 8000 rpm)

Current value: 108 (6.59 mS, 82.4%)

New value: 108

OK   Cancel

The **'Block map functions'** for the injection map are **'Fill'**, **'Add'**, **'Subtract'**, **'Increase by %'** and **'Decrease by %'**.

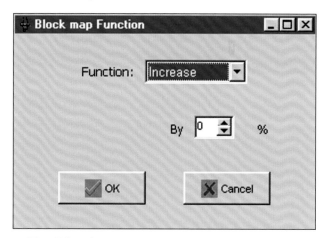

The PC software can also calculate map settings between two settings/sites on the map. This can be a very useful aid to speed up the mapping process. For example, if you have mapped two points, say at load-site 5 and then load-site 7, you can use the PC control software to 'guess' the setting at load-site 6 by interpolating between sites 5 and 7. To do this, block a column between sites 5 and 7 and press **'C'** (for calculate). The numbers changed by this function will be highlighted blue with the mapped numbers being red. It is a good idea to check these 'guessed' sites when mapping on a dyno or rolling road.

The software will calculate over any number of load or speed sites using the end points of the highlighted block with linear interpolation between sites. You often find that there are areas of the map where you do need to map every site, eg around very light throttle where a small change in throttle angle results in a large change in air flow. Progress is usually slow when starting a map, and this function allows you to map a few sites and quickly get a sensible map into shape by filling in the gaps; you can then go back over interpolated sites to check/fine-tune them.

Below is an example using this function. Load sites 3 and 5 were mapped (numbers highlighted red). You can see that the number at load site 4 is obviously too high. The calculate function is used to replace the number at load site 4 with one that is between the values of load sites 3 and 5.

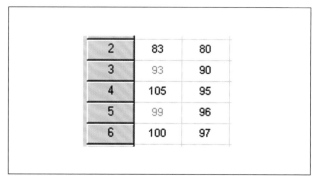

1. Load sites 3 and 5 mapped.

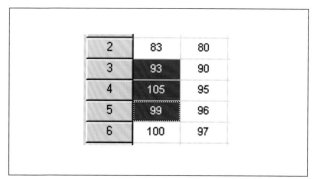

2. Block column.

3. Press 'C' to calculate between sites 3 and 5.

4. Result, calculated/interpolated value at load site 4.

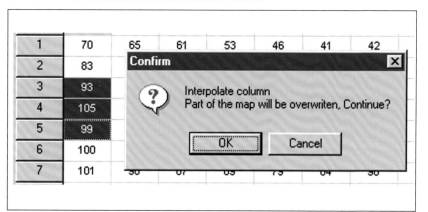

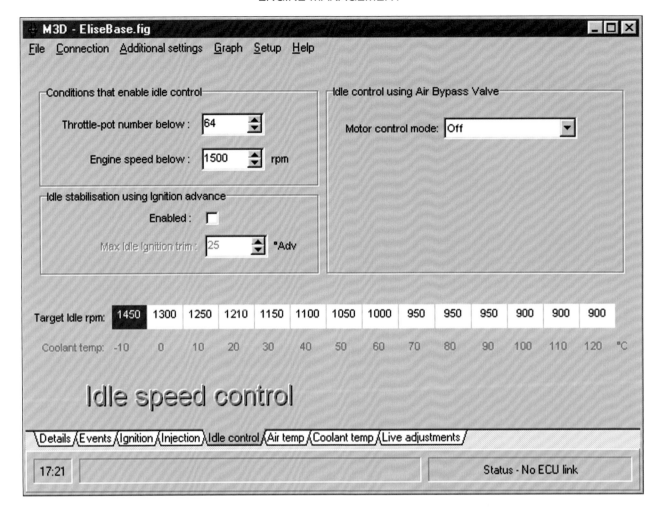

'Idle control' (F5)

A stable idle speed can normally be achieved with correct ignition and injection settings in the main maps. The first thing to remember is that, when at idle, the inlet air speed will fall as the rpm is reduced. With a lower inlet air speed, less fuel will be carried through into the cylinder, as fuel drops out of the air stream. The amount of fuel drop-out will depend on various factors such as fuel-injector spray (atomisation), air temperature, distance of injector from cylinder, etc. To counter this fuel drop-out, the fuel-injection numbers will normally be increased below the idle speed sites (see a base map for an example, most have an idle speed close to speed site 2).

Without knowing this, it is often assumed that as the rpm decreases the fuel demand decreases (or at least remains the same). This will usually result in an engine that is prone to stalling – if the idle speed falters, for whatever reason, the air speed falls, fuel drops out of the air stream, the mixture becomes lean, the idle speed drops further, air speed falls more, and so on...

Another trick to produce a stable idle is to use the ignition map to ramp up the ignition timing if the idle speed falls to a site below that you wish to be idling at. For example, you may have an idle speed of 1,000rpm (speed site 2), and an ignition advance of 5° in the ignition map. Putting an ignition value of 15° in the speed site below this (speed site 1) will mean the ECU will interpolate between these two sites and automatically advance the ignition if the rpm falls below 1,000rpm.

The ECU has optional **'Idle stabilisation using ignition advance'** and **'Idle control using air bypass valve'** functions that can be used to give a stable idle under varying conditions. For these functions to be used, the ECU needs to be able to determine when the engine is actually in an idle condition. The engine is normally said to be idling when the engine speed is below a certain rpm and the throttle is shut. The **'Conditions that enable idle control'** values allow the ECU to determine when the engine is in the idle condition.

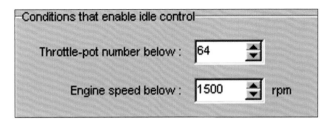

You can see in this example that when the throttle-pot number is below 64 **and** the engine rpm is below 1500rpm, the idle speed conditions will be met and the ECU will enable any idle speed control functions. When these conditions have been met the **'IAC pos'** number in the **'Live adjustments'** screen will be coloured red, otherwise it will be coloured green.

To determine the **'Throttle-pot number below'** value, select **'Throttle pot'** from the **'Setup'** menu while the engine is running. You aren't going to actually complete the alignment routine, just use display to view the throttle-pot number when the engine is running. Make a note of this number, then gently press the throttle pedal until the engine rpm just starts to increase and make a note of this number. Click the **'Cancel'** button when you have finished viewing the throttle-pot number.

For example, you may have an idle speed of 1000rpm and a throttle-pot number of 60 (it may flick between, say 60 and 61). The throttle-pot number may increase to 66 before you get a noticable increase in rpm. Use a number somewhere between these two throttle-pot numbers for the **'Throttle-pot number below'** input. The idea is that you want the ECU to relinquish control of the idle as soon as you touch the throttle pedal. You also don't want this threshold so close to the throttle-shut pot number that the fluctuations in the throttle-pot number (due to voltage stability, temperature, vibration, etc) constantly enable/disable the idle control functions.

Once the idle condition has been determined the **'Idle stabilisation using ignition advance'** function, if enabled, will be activated.

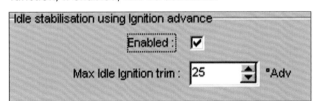

Once enabled and activated, this function will rapidly increase the ignition advance in 0.5° steps if the engine rpm is below that determined by the **'Target idle rpm'** table. The function can only increase the ignition advance, it will **not** retard the base ignition advance if the idle speed is too high. The **'Max idle ignition trim'** value determines how much this function is allowed to advance the ignition in order to reach the target rpm. Under certain conditions advancing the ignition timing alone is not enough to increase the idle speed to reach the target rpm. Without the **'Max idle ignition trim'** value the function would continue to advance the ignition until it was too far advanced to run, and the engine would stall.

Tip: *If you intend to use this* **'Idle stabilisation using ignition advance'** *function it is a good idea to leave it disabled until the mapping work is finished. Use a very retarded idle speed ignition timing in the base map, eg 0°–10°, and when the engine is hot set the idle to the desired idle speed using the throttle stop screw. With this low advance in the base map you will need to have the throttle in a more open position, this will give more cylinder filling which in turn will mean that an increase in ignition advance will have more of an effect on the idle speed, and therefore the idle-stabilisation function will be more effective.*

The **'Target idle rpm'** table (see illustration below) is used by the **'Idle stabilisation using ignition advance'** function to determine the engine speed that is desired for a given coolant temperature. The ECU will use the coolant temperature to 'look up' the target idle rpm for that temperature. This target rpm is then compared with the actual engine rpm. If the engine rpm is below the target rpm the ignition timing is increased in steps (up to the maximum allowed trim) until the engine speed and target speed match. Unless an air bypass valve is also used in conjunction with this function, it may not be possible for the target rpm to be reached.

As this function name suggests, it should only really be relied on to provide stabilisation or fine control of the idle speed. An air bypass valve would normally be used to provide a slow-responding coarse idle-speed adjustment, with the stabilisation function providing a rapid-responding fine idle speed adjustment. Some applications won't have an air bypass valve so the stabilisation function can be used on its own to give a good improvement to the idle quality under varying conditions.

Target Idle rpm:	1450	1300	1250	1210	1150	1100	1050	1000	950	950	950	900	900	900	
Coolant temp:	-10	0	10	20	30	40	50	60	70	80	90	100	110	120	°C

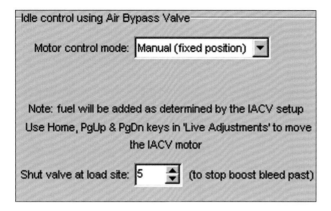

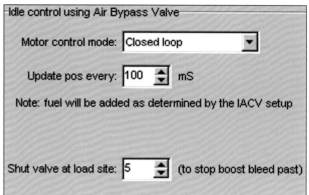

The **'Idle control using air bypass valve'** settings determine the way the air bypass motor is controlled. With the **'Motor control mode'** set to **'Off'** the ECU will completely disable any outputs associated with the control of the IACV (idle air control valve), and any corrections to the maps from associated look up tables will be ignored.

With the **'Motor control mode'** set to **'Fixed position (manual control)'** – see illustration above – the IACV position can be controlled directly from the keyboard when in the **'Live adjustments'** (F8) screen. The motor position will be 'remembered', so the motor will remain at this position even when the ECU is powered up next.

As the IACV is an ECU-controlled air leak, and the fuelling is primarily determined by throttle position, this extra air will go undetected and will result in the mixture going lean. There is another look-up table that enables you to map in extra fuel to compensate for the extra air introduced by the IACV. This table is found in the **'Additional settings – Idle Air Control'** screen.

With the **'Motor control mode'** set to **'Mapped position'** (Closed loop) the IACV position is controlled by the ECU only, and the keyboard control of the motor is disabled (see illustration above). The IACV position is now determined by a small look-up table found in the **'Additional settings – Idle Air Control'** screen. The ECU will move the IACV to a preset start-up position as soon as the ignition is switched on. If the target rpm has been reached, the IACV position will be close to the position determined by the **'Base IACV position'** table. Refer to the 'Idle Air Control' section later in this chapter for more information on these settings.

In some pressure-charged engine applications it is possible for boost pressure to bypass the engine through the IACV and plumbing, which may then require a one-way valve to be installed. If the **'Motor control mode'** is set to **'Fixed position (manual control)'** or **'Mapped position'**, then the ECU can be instructed to fully shut the IACV at and above a certain throttle position/site by setting the **'Shut valve at load site x'** to a non-zero value. Once the load site has reached this value, the current valve position will be remembered and the valve will then be fully shut. As soon as the load site falls below this threshold value the valve will be returned to its previous position and will operate as before.

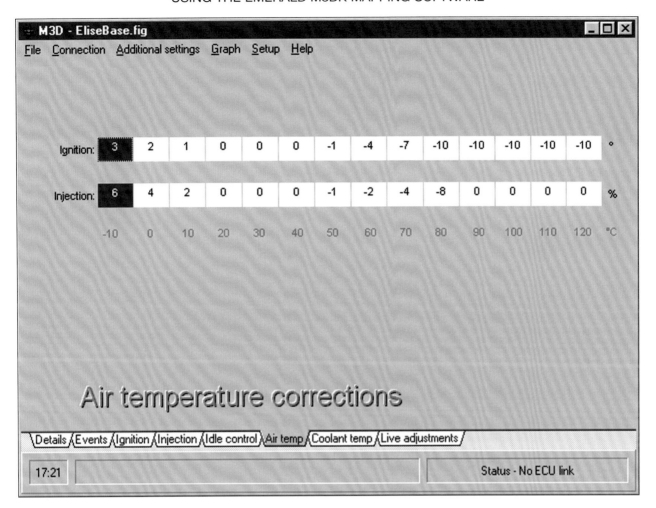

'Air temp' (F6)

The density of the inlet charge varies with inlet air temperature. This varying density changes the amount of oxygen trapped in the cylinder, and will therefore change the air/fuel mixture ratio. For every 10°C increase in inlet temperature the density of the air is reduced by approximately 3%, therefore the fuel injected will need to be reduced by the same percentage in order to maintain a constant air/fuel mixture ratio.

A standard temperature of 20° C is usually used, at which point there is no correction to the injection pulse width. Below this temperature the fuelling is increased (corrected up) and above this temperature the fuelling is reduced (corrected down).

The change in inlet air density also effectively changes the cylinder filling, so the ignition timing requirements will also change slightly. More importantly though, with increasing inlet air temperature there is more chance of detonation/pinking due to increasing cylinder temperatures. It is common to retard the ignition timing slightly as the inlet air temperature increases as a safety measure to protect the engine.

The injection correction and ignition correction values displayed in the **'Temperatures'** panel on the **'Live adjustments'** screen will show the actual corrections applied to the injection or ignition. The corrections displayed are those from the air temperature and the coolant temperature tables combined together.

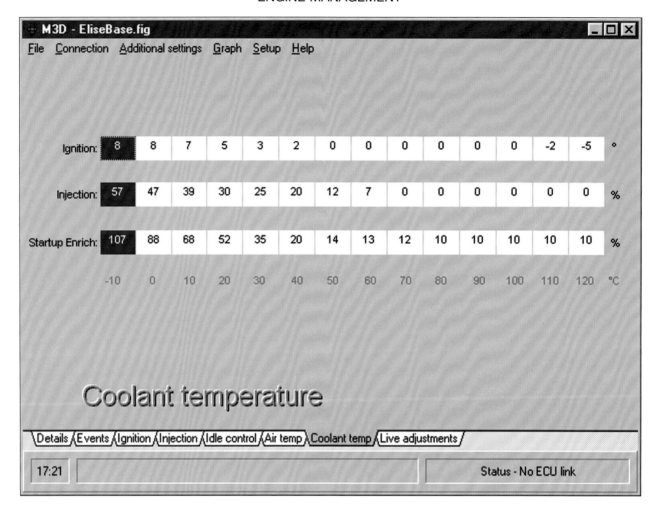

Ignition:	8	8	7	5	3	2	0	0	0	0	0	0	-2	-5	°
Injection:	57	47	39	30	25	20	12	7	0	0	0	0	0	0	%
Startup Enrich:	107	88	68	52	35	20	14	13	12	10	10	10	10	10	%
	-10	0	10	20	30	40	50	60	70	80	90	100	110	120	°C

Coolant temperature

\Details /Events /Ignition /Injection /Idle control /Air temp /Coolant temp /Live adjustments /

17:21   Status - No ECU link

'Coolant temp' (F7)

The **'Ignition'** correction table allows you to adjust the ignition timing for different engine temperatures. A cold engine may benefit from slightly more timing advance, which will often help to maintain an idle speed. To help reduce the risk of detonation, the ignition timing can be retarded at the higher temperature sites above normal.

The **'Injection'** correction table allows you to set a fuel enrichment amount, dependent on water temperature. This is very important for starting and cold running – it is the choke mechanism of the fuel injection system. Adjustment is carried out by entering a simple percentage number against coolant temperature, with full interpolation between the settings. Consider this setting as giving the engine full choke for starting, then backing the choke lever off as the engine warms up. However, you also have the facility to alter the fuelling at very high temperatures; for example, adding a fuel enrichment percentage to reduce combustion-chamber temperatures in an overheating engine.

The **'Startup Enrich'** correction table allows you to set an extra enrichment that is only applied while the engine is cranking. This extra enrichment is halved the moment the engine starts (engine rpm above 500rpm) and the remainder of the enrichment is gradually faded away over a number of seconds.

Tip. *Don't spend too much time fine tuning these enrichment tables until you have finished mapping the injection system for your application; the correction values from these injection correction tables are applied to the main map. It is very easy to be confused into adjusting the wrong coolant injection correction table. The* **'Injection'** *table value is applied to the main map at all times whereas the* **'Startup Enrich'** *table value is only applied during cranking and for a few seconds after.*

Once the injection has been mapped, allow the engine to cool fully (ideally overnight) to enable a cold start. If you have difficulty starting the engine, check the condition of the spark plugs, as they may have become fouled if the mixture is way too rich. Renew or clean the plugs if necessary. While cranking, you can increase/reduce the fuelling from the **'Live**

adjustments' screen (using the **'1'**, **'2'**, **'3'** keys). When the engine is up and running, clear any trim you may have by pressing the **'1'** key. Allow any cranking enrichment remaining to fade away – this may take a few seconds.

Check how the engine runs and revs; if the mixture is over-lean you will normally notice a poor pick-up response when you open the throttle, or 'spitting' in the inlet. If the mixture is over-rich you will normally have black smoke from the exhaust, the spark plugs will have a tendency to foul and if excessively rich the engine will be sound rough when the throttle is opened. Use the **'2'** or **'3'** key while in the **'Live**

adjustments' screen and check for an improvement. If you need to make a change to the mixture, note the temperature and stop the engine. Increase or decrease the value in the **'Injection'** correction table at the appropriate temperature site. Reprogram the ECU with the changes and repeat the process.

Note: *Keep a careful eye on the water temperature as you adjust the enrichment. The engine heats up quite quickly, and you might find yourself adding fuel at a given temperature, not having noticed that the engine temperature has moved on. This process may take some time, and it may be necessary to carry out a few cold-starts to get the correction table spot on.*

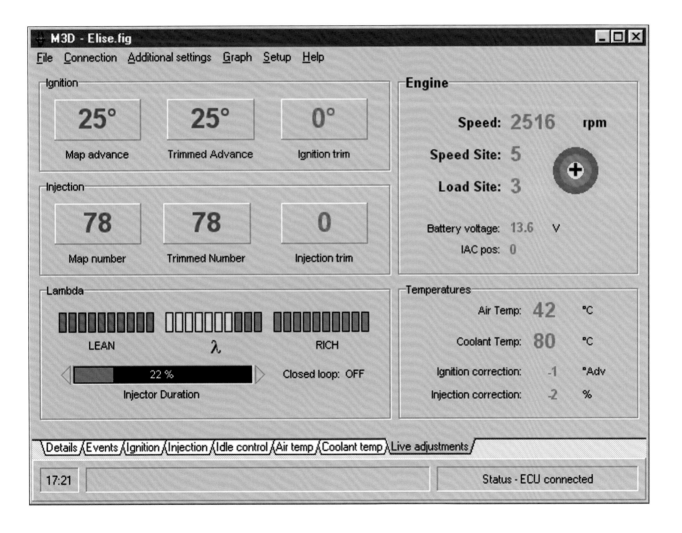

'Live adjustments' (F8)

This page displays the current live information the ECU is working with. This information shows you the engine data inputs that the ECU has measured, and also the mapping information that results from these inputs.

The page is split up into 5 titled panels to make the information easier to understand (see illustration on previous page). These are:

1   Engine
2   Temperatures
3   Ignition
4   Injection
5   Lambda

1 'Engine'

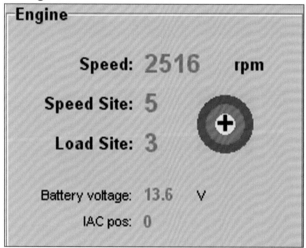

This panel shows the basic engine running condition. The engine **'Speed'** (rpm) is displayed and also the current **'Speed site'** that this rpm falls into. The current speed site ranges from 0 to 31, and references the ignition and injection maps to engine speed. Each speed site covers a range of engine rpm, eg 1000 to 1500rpm = 500rpm.

The indicated **'Load site'** is determined by the throttle position; as the throttle is opened the number should rise. If the throttle pot has been correctly set-up using the throttle pot alignment procedure, the load site should range from 0 (throttle fully closed) to 15 (throttle fully open).

The cross on the target shows the level of interpolation between speed/load sites. With the cross in the middle of the target there is no interpolation between sites – the injection/ignition values are only determined by the one map cell, as indicated by the current speed and load sites. As the rpm increases slightly the cross will move to the right showing that the ECU is interpolating between the current site and the map cell at the next speed site. The cross will move vertically to indicate interpolation with sites above/below the current load site.

This is very useful when mapping. You want to have the target as close to the middle as possible so you know that you are just trimming that one particular site and the actual injection/ignition output is not also being affected by another map cell value. When you press **'Enter'** to store a trimmed map value, only the one cell at the current speed/load site is changed. Ensuring that you have the cross in the centre at that time means the new untrimmed map will produce the same injection/ignition output as the previously trimmed map.

The displayed **'Battery voltage'** should indicate approx 13–14.5 volts when the alternator is charging. If the battery voltage is showing higher or lower than this, the alternator condition should be checked. Also, the battery voltage can be monitored while cranking – a very low voltage may seriously impair the performance of the coil/injectors etc, and make starting difficult. A battery voltage of 9-10 volts while cranking is normal, and the cranking voltage needs to be a minimum of 6 volts for the ECU to operate.

The **'IAC pos'** number indicates the current position of the idle air control valve (if fitted). The colour of this number also indicates whether the ECU has determined the engine is idling, and therefore whether the idle control functions are being allowed to operate (if they are enabled). If the **'IAC pos'** number is coloured red, the ECU is in idle control mode, otherwise the number is coloured green. The engine rpm and the throttle pot number are used by the ECU to determine if the engine is idling – these settings are found in the **'Idle speed control'** screen (F5).

Depending on the current operating mode of the IAC valve, the valve can be moved manually using the keyboard from the **'Live adjustments'** screen. Pressing **'Home'** will move the valve to the fully closed position (IAC pos: 0). Pressing the **'Page Up'** or **'Page Down'** keys (**'PgUp'**/**'PgDn'**) will open/close the valve by one step. Pressing the **'Shift'** key at the same time as **'Page Up'** or **'Page Down'** will move the motor in steps of 10.

2 'Temperatures'

Temperatures		
Air Temp: 42	°C	
Coolant Temp: 80	°C	
Ignition correction: -1	°Adv	
Injection correction: -2	%	

The **'Air temp'** figure shows the current inlet air temperature measurement in degrees centigrade.

The **'Coolant temp'** figure shows the current engine coolant temperature measurement in degrees centigrade.

If either the coolant or air temperature sensors are disconnected, or the reading is out of range, the reading will be highlighted as shown in the example below.

The **'Ignition correction'** shows you how much the basic ignition timing (as determined by the ignition map, speed site and load site) is being altered due to temperature correction. This value is the combined result of both the air and coolant corrections – eg, at an air temperature of 40°C the correction may be –2° but at the same time the coolant temperature of 105° may be correcting the ignition timing by –1°. The displayed correction value will be –3°.

Usually the temperature-based ignition correction is used to reduce the risk of pinking/detonation at extreme coolant/air temperatures. A high inlet-air charge temperature makes the engine more prone to detonation, so the ignition timing is often retarded as a safety measure. Also, a very high coolant temperature can mean increased combustion-chamber temperatures that may lead to pinking/detonation, so the ignition may be retarded to reduce that risk.

The displayed **'Injection correction'** value is derived in exactly the same way. It is a combination of the coolant temperature correction and air temperature correction, but does not include the accel fuelling correction or the cranking enrichment.

Under normal conditions the injection correction value will be a positive value that decreases as the coolant temperature increases. When the engine reaches normal running temperature, the correction will be zero. Because the density of the air entering the engine (and therefore the volume of oxygen) varies with the inlet air temperature, the injected fuel quantity can be corrected to maintain a constant mixture ratio. As the inlet temperature rises, the density of the air reduces, and if the injected fuel quantity is not corrected the mixture will become richer. Also, the reverse is true; a cool inlet-air charge temperature means a denser inlet charge (more oxygen), so the mixture will become lean.

Note: *The map values that compensate for air temperature/injection correction do not normally need to be altered; the relationship is constant regardless of engine. Most base maps supplied on*

disk will have these values pre-set, although they can be zeroed if an air temperature sensor is not used.

3 'Ignition'

The basic ignition timing, which is determined by the ignition map and referenced by the speed/load sites, is displayed in the first box titled **'Map advance'**. The ignition timing can be advanced or retarded in 1° steps from the keyboard when this live adjustments screen is showing. The current ignition advance trim that has been applied by you is shown in the box titled **'Ignition trim'** and is coloured red. The **'Trimmed advance'** box shows you the result of the basic ignition advance and the trimmed advance.

The **'0'**, **'–'**, and **'+'** keys (on the main keyboard, not the numeric keypad) can be used to trim the ignition advance while the engine is running:

'0' (zero key) Clears the current trim – the ignition timing returns to that derived from the map only (ie, the ignition timing the engine was running before it was trimmed from the keyboard).

'–' (minus key) Retards (trims) the ignition timing by 1°.

'+' (plus key) Advances (trims) the ignition timing by 1°.

If you find that the trimmed ignition advance is preferred, you can make a note of the advance you have at the current load/speed site, switch to the ignition map screen (**'F3'** key) and enter the number in the map at the same site. You will then need to program the ECU with the new settings for them to take effect (**'Program ECU'** item from the **'Connection'** drop-down menu).

Tip: *It is always a good idea to save the current map stored in the ECU to disk before you make any changes. This way can you always re-install the original settings if you lose your way. To retrieve the current map stored in the ECU, select the* **'Read ECU'** *item from the* **'Connection'** *drop-down menu. To then store this map to disk, select the* **'Save Map File'** *item from the* **'File'** *drop-down menu.*

Another way to store your trimmed advance in the map is to press **'Enter'** when at the speed/load site you want to change. When you press **'Enter'**, this trimmed advance will be programmed into the ECU's map at the speed/load site you selected. The ECU's map will now be changed in the same way it would have been if you had used the previous method. The map advance will now be what was the trimmed advance. The ignition trim value will be automatically zeroed to prevent the newly programmed map site being trimmed again. At the same time the map site in the ECU is programmed, the map stored in the PC will also be programmed. Both the map store in the ECU and the PC will be the same. If you switch to the ignition map (**'F3'**) you will see that the programmed site will be coloured red to indicate that this site was programmed from the live adjustments screen.

4 'Injection'

The basic fuel injection quantity is determined by the injection map and referenced by the speed/load sites. The number that represents this quantity is displayed in the first box titled **'Map number'** and ranges from 0 (no fuel) to 255 (max fuel). The fuel injection quantity can be increased or reduced in steps of 1 from the keyboard when this live adjustments screen is showing. The current injection trim that has been applied by you is shown in the box titled **'Injection trim'** and is coloured red. The **'Trimmed number'** box shows you the result of the basic map number and the trimmed number.

The **'1'**, **'2'**, and **'3'** keys (on the main keyboard, not the numeric keypad) are used to trim the fuel map number while the engine is running:

- **'1'** Clears the current trim – the fuel injection quantity returns to that derived from the map only (ie, the injection map number the engine was running before it was trimmed from the keyboard).
- **'2'** Reduces (trims) the map fuel number by 1.
- **'3'** Increase (trims) the map fuel number by 1.

As with the ignition trim, the injection trimmed number can be programmed into the ECU map by either manually changing the injection map at the desired load/speed site and then selecting the **'Program ECU'** item from the **'Connection'** drop down menu, **or** by pressing **'Enter'**. Pressing **'Enter'** will program the injection map at the current speed/load with the trimmed injection number.

Note: *The engine will not need to have been stopped before selecting* **'Program ECU'**.

Tip: *It is always a good idea to save the current map stored in the ECU to disk before you make any changes. This way can you always re-install the original settings if you lose your way. To retrieve the current map stored in the ECU, select the* **'Read ECU'** *item from the* **'Connection'** *drop-down menu. To*

then store this map to disk, select the **'Save Map File'** item from the **'File'** drop-down menu.

5 'Lambda'

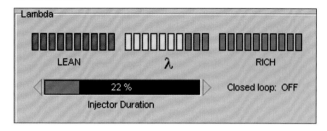

If fitted with a lambda sensor, the 30 red/yellow/green 'LEDs' give you a visual representation of the sensor's output signal. This display can be very useful when mapping, as it gives you a very quick indication of the fuel mixture.

Lambda sensors need to operate at a minimum temperature. The output may take from a few seconds to a few minutes to react while the sensor heats up – this time depends on engine temperature, engine load, distance from sensor to engine, etc. Many sensors are now electrically heated, which greatly reduces the time taken to give an output signal.

A Lambda sensor is really only a switch which switches from lean/rich at an air/fuel ratio of 14.7:1 (stoichemetric), and can only accurately indicate a lean or a rich mixture.

At the switching point there is some slope to the output signal which will give an output that is, to some extent, proportional to the air/fuel ratio, but this slope will change depending on various variables such as sensor age, sensor condition and exhaust temperature. Therefore this display should not be used as exact measurement, but it can be a very useful guide. Accurate mixture ratios need to be measured with an expensive wide-band lambda sensor that requires additional interface circuitry.

Exhaust analysers can also be used, but their reaction time makes their use very limited.

As a *rough* guide, the lambda signal should be somewhere in the green segment of the display when running a power mixture ratio (rich, high-load throttle positions), and somewhere in the red segment of the display for economy (lean, light throttle positions).

Information relevant to the lambda display is also close by. The injection duration bar shows you how hard the injectors are being worked. The ECU calculates the percentage of the available time the injectors are on for (duration %), and this is displayed in the duration bar. At the extremes of injector duration, ie very short or long opening pulse, the duration bar changes colour as a warning. Below 10% duration the bar will turn yellow. Above 85% duration the bar will turn red, and at or above 100% the triangular LED to the right of the bar will flash red/yellow.

At the extremes of duration the turn on/off characteristics of the injector have a greater effect on the accuracy of the quantity of fuel injected. This isn't such an issue with the way the M3DK system works (where the pulse width is directly determined by look-up tables, rather than calculated in order to give a measured quantity of fuel). It is a good idea to size your injectors, or set the fuel pressure, so that you are making best use of the injectors' flow rate. Ideally you want the maximum duration to be approx 85–90%. Using injectors that are too big will mean that the injector pulse widths will be smaller, and at around idle speed the resolution of the injector pulse may make it difficult to get a good exhaust mixture. If you find that the injectors are too small, you can check/increase the fuel pressure to provide more fuel flow. Fuel pressure should normally be in the region of 2.5 to 4.0 bar – fuel atomisation, spray pattern and other factors means it is advisable to keep the fuel pressure in this region. Using the **'Injection Scaling'** function (see later in this Chapter) will enable the system to re-scale the map to compensate for changes you may want to make to the fuel pressure or injector size, without requiring a complete re-map of the system.

Additional settings

'Accel fuelling'

This is the electronic equivalent of the accelerator-pump jet system found on a carburettor. It allows a percentage of fuel to be added automatically when the ECU detects a certain rate of throttle pedal movement. Change the **'Accel enrichment'** number, and keep playing until you have the minimum amount of accel fuelling that will prevent any flat spot on snap throttle opening. The **'Accel clamp'** number determines how long the enrichment is applied before it starts decaying. You can also change the **'Accel decay'** rate. This is the speed at which the accel fuelling drops away. Simply select the lowest value that prevents any hiccups after initial snap throttle opening during road testing.

Important note: *Do not try to use this facility to mask a weak spot in the main fuelling map. If the main jet in a carb was weak you wouldn't, or shouldn't, try to mask it by fitting a larger accelerator pump jet. Get the main map setting right before you worry about accel fuel settings.*

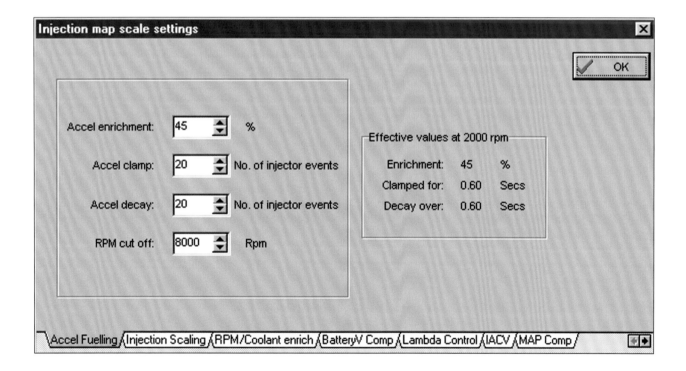

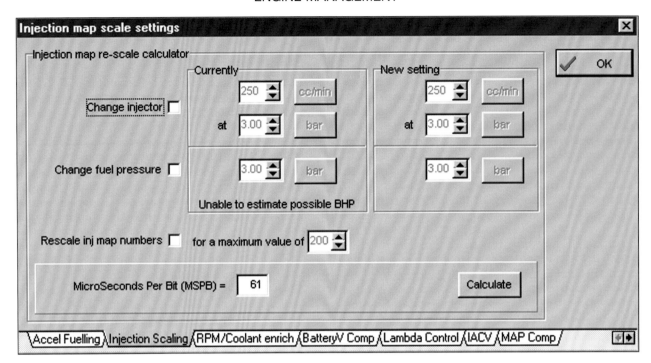

'Injection scaling'

The basis of the injector pulse width is the number stored in the injection map. This is just a number between 0 and 255. This injection number is manipulated and corrected for various things such as temperature, pressure, etc, but is still just a number. The ECU scales this number using the **'MicroSeconds Per Bit (MSPB)'** value to convert the number into a pulse-width time. The MSPB value is the number of microseconds (0.000001 seconds, 'µS') each unit of the injection number represents. Eg, an injection number of 100 and an MSPB of 61 equates to a pulse width of 100 x 61µS = 6100µS. Injector pulse widths are normally shown in milliseconds (0.001 seconds, mS). In this example the final pulse width would be 6.1mS.

The MSPB has a default value of 61, although this can be changed to give you finer control of the injector pulse width but the maximum pulse width possible will be reduced. There are a number of functions on this screen that will manipulate the MSPB value, so normally there is no need to change this number directly.

The injection map can be rescaled to cater for a change in fuel pressure or injector size. You may find during a mapping session that the injectors are too small or the fuel pressure needs increasing to give increased fuel flow. Quite often a lot of work has been done with the map by the time it is discovered that you need more fuel flow. By rescaling the injection map using the MSPB value to suit the new fuel pressure/injector size, you can carry on where you left off with very little additional work needed.

'Change injector'
Select the **'Change injector'** check box to enable the injector settings. If known, enter the current injector flow rate and test pressure (normally supplied by the injector manufacturer) in the **'Currently'** boxes. *These flow figures are stored in the ECU along with the map, but they are not stored with the map on disk.* After an injector change, select the **'Change injector'** check box, then enter the new injector flow rate and test pressure in the **'New setting'** boxes. The flow/pressure units can be imperial or metric, just select the button displaying the current units to toggle between them. Once the new figures have been entered, click the **'Calculate'** button. The MSPB value needed to scale the injection map to produce the same fuel flow with the new injectors will then be calculated. Once the ECU is reprogrammed with the new settings (carried out by selecting **'Connection'/'Program ECU'**) the engine should run just as it did with the original settings and injectors, but with the new fuel capacity (the injection duration bar in the **'Live adjustments'** screen will reflect this).

'Change fuel pressure'
Just as with the **'Change injector'** function you can select this check box to enter your current settings to be saved in the ECU with the map. The MSPB value will only be changed if there is a difference in the current and new settings, and you have clicked the **'Calculate'** button. With the ECU connected and powered, the control software will know the number

of cylinders of the engine, and with the injector flow rate/fuel pressure information, the approximate maximum BHP will be displayed. This gives you an idea of how much power can be achieved using the selected injector size/fuel pressure.

'Rescale inj map numbers'
As the injection numbers range from 0–255, it can be seen that if you end up with a map that only spans 100 of these you are losing out on resolution. By rescaling the injection map numbers and MSPB, this function will keep the fuel injection output exactly the same but increase the injection map numbers to the maximum value that you require. This will then give you more resolution, enabling you to do more fine-tuning, which may prove to be especially useful around idle and very light throttles, where you may need a very fine pulse-width resolution.

For example, with a maximum injection map number of 100, and an MSPB of 61, the maximum pulse width will be 6.1mS and each unit will be 0.061mS. When trimming the map in the **'Live adjustments'** screen, each tap of the key will change the pulse width by 0.061mS.

If you choose to rescale the injection map numbers for a maximum value of 200 (click the **'Rescale inj map numbers'** check box, set the **'for a maximum value of'** number to 200, click **'Calculate'**, then program the ECU as described previously) the MPSB will be recalculated as 30.5 and rounded to 31 (fractional values not allowed). The maximum pulse width will now be 6.2mS, and each unit will be 0.031mS. You can see that the injection resolution has doubled. Due to rounding errors, the final injection output may be affected slightly (1.5% in this case), so

the map may need to be checked.

Tip: Before using this function, make sure that any unused map sites above the maximum rpm you have mapped to are not going to affect the final scaling. These numbers may be left over from a base map you used initially. To be sure, block all the sites in the area above which the engine won't be running, and fill them with a zero figure.

'RPM correction for coolant enrichment'
When extra enrichment is added for cold running, a lot of the fuel drops out of the air flow due to the low air velocity through the port on idle. If you try to drive off while the engine is still on warm up enrichment, the resulting higher rpm increases the air velocity through the port and this in turn carries more fuel into the engine – hence it runs rich.

The answer to this is the **'RPM correction for coolant enrichment'** map. Basically this just gives you the facility to remove the excess fuel, carried to the engine due to the higher rpm, during the warm up cycle. If you take the trouble to get this map right you can drive off with a cold engine and not waste fuel through over-enrichment caused by the higher rpm.

'Battery voltage compensation'
The injectors would open at a different rate if the voltage available were to vary. The software in the system automatically alters the injector period to compensate for battery voltage changes, thus keeping the amount of fuel injected the same for all battery conditions.

'Lambda control'
Switching the Lambda control on will put the system into closed-loop mode. This alters the mixture based on Lambda sensor readings across the stoichiometric

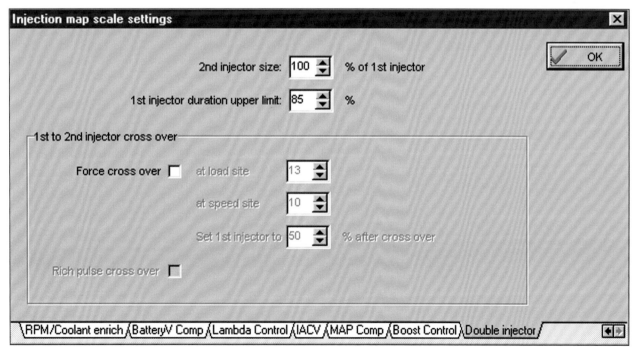

ratio for the benefit of the catalytic converter. Closed loop will only operate on light load and idle.

'Idle air control'

If the engine is fitted with an Idle Air Control Valve (IACV), this can be used for course adjustments of the idle speed. In the main this valve is used on cold starting and during warm up. On the Emerald system there is also a separate fuel map to compensate for the additional air that the IACV bleeds into the intake. In a throttle-pot-based system this is not automatically allowed for as it is when running from a Manifold Air Pressure (MAP) sensor.

Double injector control

The M3DK system can control two injectors per cylinder for up to four cylinders. Two injectors per cylinder may be used for a couple of reasons. One reason is injector sizing. Using two small injectors in place of one large injector gives you the advantage of having a small single injector for fine control of fuelling when fuel flow demands are low, as well as the option of higher fuel flow when both injectors are used together.

Another reason for using two injectors per cylinder is that the additional injector can be used to inject the fuel further up-stream in the inlet tract at high rpm, in order to get better mixture preparation, and therefore give a power increase, whilst still using the original injector in the standard position at lower rpm.

The illustration on the previous page shows the settings screen for the double injector control. In this example the **'Force cross over'** check box is unchecked, so the ECU will only operate the 2nd bank of injectors when the duration of the 1st injector bank has reached the **'1st injector duration upper limit'** of 85%. At this point the 1st bank of injectors will be clamped at this duration of 85%, and all additional fuelling will then be through the 2nd bank of injectors.

The ECU will determine the fuel needed above the limit of the 1st bank of injectors and then scale this duration using the **'2nd injector size'** value. If the

injectors of the 1st and 2nd banks are of the same size then the value for the **'2nd injector size'** should be 100%. If the 2nd bank injectors are twice the size of the first bank injectors, this value should be 200%. This method of operation is often used on pressure-charged engines with a high bhp/litre. This allows you to use small injectors in the 1st bank to give good fuel control at idle and low loads, with an additional bank of injectors to provide the extra fuel needed for high power output.

Some applications require an additional bank of injectors further out in the inlet tract to provide better mixture preparation for a power increase. In this case the **'Force cross over'** check box should be checked. Using the values in the above illustration as an example, the ECU would be 'forced' to activate the 2nd bank of injectors as soon as the speed site was 10 or above (5000+ rpm) and the load site was 13 or above (almost full throttle). The total amount of fuel to be injected can be divided as desired between the 1st and 2nd injector banks. The **'Set 1st injector bank to xx % after cross over'** value determines how much of the total fuel will be injected by the 1st bank injectors, the 2nd bank will inject the remainder. This example has the split at 50:50, with the 1st bank and 2nd bank each injecting half the total amount of fuel. The 2nd injector bank pulse width is still scaled using the **'2nd injector size'** value to allow for different sizes of injector.

When the **'Force cross over'** option is used, the double injector function will still operate as before using the **'1st injector upper limit'** value but, depending on injector sizing and application, this upper limit value may never come in to effect – eg a normally aspirated engine using outer injectors may have 1st and 2nd injector banks of the same size, each capable of supplying all of the fuel needed, so this upper limit is never reached.

The total injector duration of the 1st and 2nd banks is calculated when the ECU is operating double injectors. The injector duration bar in the **'Live adjustments'** screen changes to indicate that the

1st to 2nd injector cross over

Force cross over ☑ at load site `13`

at speed site `10`

Set 1st injector to `50` % after cross over

Rich pulse cross over ☐

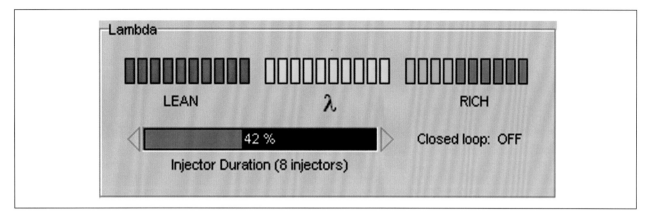

double injection function is active, and the duration % shows that of both injector banks combined.

Note: *The ECU will only operate the double injector function if the '**Injection output**' setting in the '**ECU configuration**' screen (selected from the '**Setup**' menu) is set to '**Grouped/double injectors**'.*

*Tip: If you don't have the flow rate values for the injectors in the 1st and 2nd injector banks in order to set the '**2nd injector size**' value, then with the injectors still plumbed to the fuel rail and pulled back from the inlet manifold, put a test tube or a similar small container (if not a graduated test tube) under one injector of each bank. Power the fuel pump, then switch on both injectors (disconnect the relevant injectors from the car's wiring loom and power them both together at the same time by connecting them directly to a 12-volt power supply). Fill the test tubes sufficiently to get a good comparison between the two injectors, and measure the level with a ruler (or use the test-tube graduations) to get the level*

*difference. The difference in level can be used to calculate the % difference between the two injectors. Eg, after 30 seconds of injection, injector A filled its tube to 50mm and injector B filled its tube to 75mm. Therefore if injector B is used in the 2nd bank, the '**2nd injector bank size**' value would be set to 150%, (75mm divided by 50mm) x 100 = 150%.*

Rover K-series immobiliser function

First time installation

For the M3DK immobiliser to function it will need to 'learn' the signal from the car's immobiliser unit. With the ignition switched on, click on the '**Immobiliser**' item from the '**Setup**' drop-down menu. The screen below will appear.

The first line shows you the current status of the ECU's immobiliser function. In this case it is

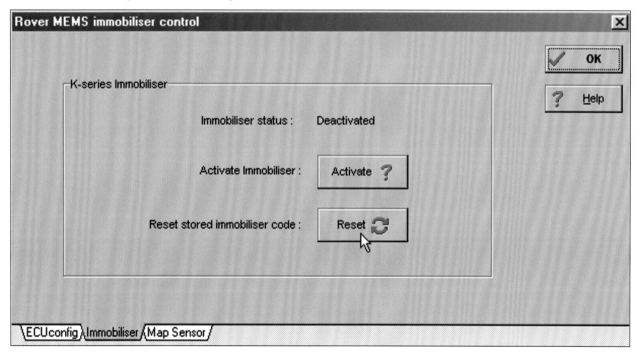

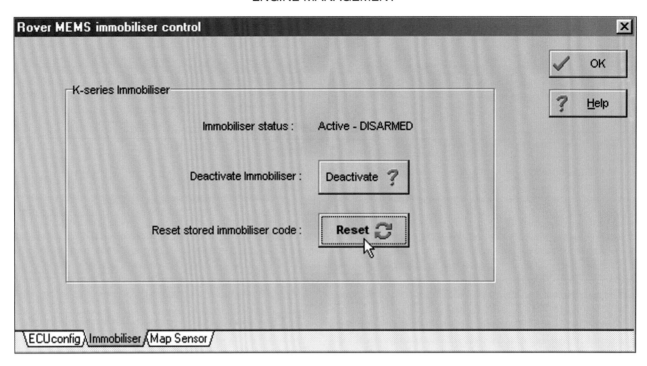

deactivated (this status information is only valid while the ECU is online).

Next, make sure that the car's immobiliser is disarmed. The Lucas 5AS unit will now be continuously transmitting a code to the ECU. To enable the M3DK system to learn this code, click the **'Reset'** button. This will erase the currently stored code and the ECU will attempt to learn another code. The immobiliser status should briefly flash **'Active – learning'** and then display **'Active – DISARMED'**, as show in the following illustration.

From now on, the ECU will be immobilised (the ECU will not react to engine rotation – ie no sparks and no injection) if the signal from the car's immobiliser is not recognised. This condition will be displayed on the Immobiliser status line as **'Active – IMMOBILISED'**.

The ECU's immobiliser function can be de-activated by clicking the **'Deactivate?'** button, this will return the immobiliser status to **'Deactivated'**.

Note: *When the immobiliser function is activated, the M3DK system will not run on any other car regardless of the car's immobiliser state. To transfer the M3DK system to another Rover car, the immobiliser function would have to be deactivated or reset to learn the new code transmitted by the new car's immobiliser.*

'Plot graph' function

The **'Plot graph'** function is selected from the **'Graph'** menu. This function simply displays a 3D visual representation of the selected map. The map to be displayed can be selected from the **'Display'** box. From the **'Zoom'** box, the map view can be enlarged or reduced by clicking the **'+'** and **'-'** buttons (**'Reset'** will return the map to its default size). The map view can be rotated and tilted by clicking and dragging the buttons at the bottom and right-hand side of the map window.

Index

Other books from Haynes Publishing

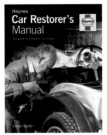

ISBN 1 85960 853 1
£17.99

ISBN 1 85960 694 6
£18.99

ISBN 1 85960 636 9
£17.99

ISBN 1 85960 962 7
£17.99

ISBN 1 85960 644 X
£19.99

ISBN 1 85960 624 5
£19.99

ISBN 1 85960 662 8
£19.99

ISBN 1 85960 653 9
£19.99

ISBN 1 85960 866 3
£17.99

ISBN 1 85960 619 9
£17.99

ISBN 1 85960 435 8
£17.99

ISBN 1 85960 691 1
£25.00

ISBN 1 85960 620 2
£19.99

ISBN 0 85429 933 5
£17.99

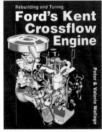

ISBN 1 85010 938 9
£17.99

ISBN 1 85960 006 9
£17.99

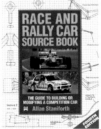

ISBN 1 85960 846 9
£19.99

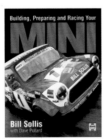

ISBN 1 85960 621 0
£17.99

For more information please contact:
Customer Services Department,
Haynes Publishing, Sparkford, Yeovil, Somerset
BA22 7JJ, UK

Tel: 01963 442030 Fax: 01963 440001
Int. tel: +44 1963 442030 Fax: +44 1963 440001

E-mail: sales@haynes.co.uk
Web site: www.haynes.co.uk